Revised and Enlarged Edition

weekendLearning
Series

# Islamic Studies

## Level 3

Mansur Ahmad and Husain A. Nuri

weekend
**Learning**

ISBN:   978-1-936569-59-5


First edition:     2008
Second edition:  2009
Third edition:    2010
Fourth edition:  2011
Reprint:          2013, 2015, 2016, 2017
Revised and enlarged edition: 2018
Reprint:          2018, 2019, 2021, 2022 (twice)

Cover Design and Photography: Mansur Ahmad
Illustrations:  Abira Das, Mansur Ahmad, Husain A. Nuri


Published in the USA by:
Weekend Learning Publishers
5584 Boulder Crest St.
Columbus, OH 43235
www.weekendlearning.com


Printed in China

# Preface

The concept of a series of Islamic Studies books was conceived in 2002 when both of us were teachers or principals of two weekend schools in two different states. We used several excellent textbooks and reference books in these schools. However, we soon realized there was no single textbook available that could meet our classroom needs. Some of the available books had too many or too few lessons for an academic year. Some lessons were too long for a class hour, and some were too short. Some lessons were too difficult for the ages involved or too basic for higher-level classes. Some books were not written with a 12 year curriculum in mind. The lessons in higher grades, therefore, did not develop from the knowledge base of prior years. Sometimes, extra emphasis was placed on one topic at the cost of other important topics. Thus, we thought a balanced knowledge base was lost.

We always felt there was a better way. We began writing the lessons ourselves to meet the needs of our schools. We involved other teachers in this process. For the next two years, we conducted classes based on the lessons we had prepared. In the meantime, both of us met with other principals and teachers across the country. We wanted to find out how they taught Islamic Studies and what their major concerns were. Most of the principals and teachers we talked to expressed their inability to find or develop a good curriculum. If they had a curriculum, they could not find lessons to complement the curriculum.

This survey prompted us to develop a functional, comprehensive curriculum for weekend schools in the West. We wanted to create a curriculum that would include everything that Muslim students growing up in the West would ideally need to know. We wanted to include topics based on the life experiences of students growing up in the West. Muslim children growing up in the U.S., Europe, and Australia are facing diverse challenges and conflicting pressures at schools and in social circles. They are constantly influenced by the mainstream youth culture. We wanted lessons to address their issues from their perspectives.

The curriculum alone would not be of any use unless there were lessons based on the curriculum. The lessons had to be age-appropriate and suitable for the typical class duration of most schools. As we continued to write and edit lessons over the next two years, we discovered ways to make the curriculum increasingly meaningful.

In 2007, we published coil-bound versions of these books. More than 30 schools in the U.S. and UK used the books. We also received a large number of inquiries from many other schools. Based on the suggestions, comments, and reviews received from many of these schools, we have edited the series of books and made other changes as appropriate.

We are thankful to Allāhﷻ for giving us the ability to write these books. We pray to Allāhﷻ to accept our labor and make us successful in communicating the message of Islam. We hope Islamic schools and home schools in the U.S. and other countries will find these books useful. Any errors in the books are our responsibility. We appreciate receiving meaningful comments and suggestions to improve the series.

*"Our Rabb! Accept from us, you indeed are the all-Hearing, all-Knowing."* (2:127)

Columbus, OH                                     Mansur Ahmad
January 15, 2008                                Husain A. Nuri

# Preface to the Revised and Enlarged Edition

All praise is due to Allāh﷾ alone. We are indebted to Him for giving us time, energy, and resources to publish this book and other books in this series. The first edition of the book was published in 2008. Over the next 10 years, we made small editorial changes in some of the lessons. During this time, our books became one of the most sought-after series all over the world for teaching Islam in weekend schools. Thousands of schools on all the continents adopted our series, and we are indebted to the teachers, students, and above all, to almighty God.

We do not want to remain idle with the success of the series. We have been constantly striving to improve the books to meet the changing and growing needs of the weekend schools. Many schools wrote to us requesting additional materials in some of the lessons. In view of their requests, we have revised and enlarged all the lessons, adding more information and resources. Our utmost focus all along has been to remain extremely loyal and true to the teachings of the Qur'ān and the authentic sunnah of the Messengerﷺ. With the enlarged lessons, teachers are now equipped with many more materials, but the teaching time in class remains the same. Therefore, the challenge will be to maximize the time available in a class by getting the most out of the lessons. This will be possible only when teachers review the lessons before coming to class and prepare themselves to do their best.

We are grateful to Brenda Rusch for editing and proofreading the book. She has not only eliminated some grammatical, punctuation, and spelling errors, but also she has improved content flow, transitions, and overall organization. Saajid Akhter and Lihan Yousuf provided help with typesetting. We thank them for their service. May Allāh﷾ accept our small effort.

July 15, 2018

Husain A. Nuri
Mansur Ahmad

# Table of Contents

# How to use this book effectively
## Instructions for the teacher and parents

The lessons for the third grade Islamic Studies are designed to develop and reinforce understanding of Islam. The purpose is to make students understand the connection between the *deen* and the *dunya*. As with other books in the series, this book also starts with a few topics on Allāh, the Qur'ān, and the Hadīth. Short biography of the Nabi is introduced as a foundation from which future lessons are developed.

The teachers are encouraged to read the lesson before coming to the class. Think about how you would deliver the content of the lesson. Most of the lessons can be read out to the students as a story. Some lessons will require the teacher to explain the content of each paragraph rather than simply reading out the lesson. As far as possible use the marker board. Jot down the sub-header of each lesson on the marker board. Do not remain seated on the chair while teaching. Move around the classroom and make frequent eye contact with the students. Ask questions frequently to reinforce learning.

For maximum benefit, each lesson should be completed in one class hour. We recommend conducting a test after every fifth or sixth lesson. Now an annotated teacher's edition of this book is available. This version provides additional text, explanation, and ayāts from the Qur'ān related to the lesson. It also contains a CD-ROM featuring question banks, ready-to-print exam questions, and homework assignments in PDF and Word files. The CD-ROM also contains many of the lessons in PowerPoint format to enhance teaching efficiency.

## Homework:
Teachers are requested to regularly assign and grade homework. The time commitment for homework is about 10–15 minutes per lesson. The homework is designed to reinforce the material learned in class and to develop a regular study habit. Frequent supervision of homework by a parent will indicate that education is valued.

## Regular Interaction with the Qur'ān:
Every Muslim student should develop the habit of interacting with the Qur'ān. To complete certain homework assignments, an English translation of the Qur'ān is strongly recommended. The purpose of such homework is to build a strong connection between the student and the Qur'ān. Insha-Allāh, such homework will plant a seed in the minds of children to continue a life-long interaction with the Qur'ān.

## Teaching Respect:
From an early age, students should be taught to show respect to Allāh, His angels, and His messengers. In order to encourage respect, teachers and parents are requested to mention the following:

Whenever the word Allāh appears in the book, please add the glorification "*Subhāna-hu wa-Taʿālā.*" Whenever the word Muhammad, or other words indicating Muhammad (for example Rasūlullāh, the Prophet, or Nabi) appear, please add the prayer "*Salla-llāhu ʿalaihi wa Sallam.*" Whenever a student reads the name of a nabi or an angel, please add the prayer "*Alai-hi-s Salām.*" Students should be taught to add the prayer "*Radi-allāhu ʿan-hu*" for a khalīfah or a male companion of Rasūlullāh. For a female companion, the prayer "*Radi-allāhu ʿan-hā*" should be used. These are noted by (R) or (ra).

## Suggestions:
Please provide any suggestions, corrections, ideas, and so forth to improve this book by sending an e-mail to the publisher at info@weekendlearning.com. It is a combined effort of the publisher, authors, teachers, and parents to prepare our future ummah. May Allāh guide us all! Amin.

# Unit 1: Knowing About Allāh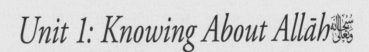

The objective of the unit is to introduce Allāh﷾ to students. While this entire book could be devoted to knowing the Creator, we can only know a little about Him. Allāh﷾ is one and the only. He is our God. He is our creator and we worship Him. Lesson 1 begins to develop these concepts and discusses many other divine characteristics. Lesson 2 discusses what Allāh﷾ is and what He is not. These questions seem simple, yet the answers offer profound information. Lesson 3 describes two of Allāh's﷾ most important attributes—His mercy and His rewards. Lesson 4 discusses another important attribute of Allāh﷾—His justice system. The final lesson in this unit focuses on some of the activities that Allāh﷾ wants us to do. The attempt here is to keep it simple, enjoyable, yet informative. If students grasp the basic ideas presented in each chapter, they will gain an understanding of Allāh﷾. The concepts introduced here are vast, but they will appear again in greater detail in future grades.

**Lesson 1:**   **Who is Allāh﷾?**

**Lesson 2:**   **What Allāh﷾ Is and Is Not**

**Lesson 3:**   **Allāh﷾:** *The Most Merciful, Most Rewarding*

**Lesson 4:**   **Allāh﷾:** *The Best Judge*

**Lesson 5:**   **What Does Allāh﷾ Want Us to Do?**

# Unit 1: Knowing About Allāh ﷻ

## Who is Allāh ﷻ?

A common question in the minds of many people is, "Who is Allāh ﷻ?" We cannot see Him, therefore, how do we learn about Him? We learn about Him by learning some of His qualities. Allāh ﷻ has given us a lot of information about Himself—His actions, His signs, His likes, and His dislikes. We also learn about Him by understanding our relationship with Him. When we learn all this information, we learn about Him.

## What Allāh ﷻ Is and Is Not

If everyone in the world fully understood what Allāh ﷻ is and is not, then everyone would probably become Muslim. A large number of people in the world do not know much about Allāh ﷻ, therefore, they make images of God and worship these images. We do not need to imagine anything about Allāh ﷻ. We simply want to learn about Him from the information He provided in the Qur'ān. This lesson provides the important information we should know.

## Allāh ﷻ: *The Most Merciful, Most Rewarding*

One of Allāh's ﷻ most significant qualities is His mercy. Allāh's ﷻ mercy covers everything. Allāh ﷻ is also the most Rewarding. Does everybody receive rewards, or are there certain criteria to receive them? Students will learn why Allāh ﷻ is so merciful and how His mercy and rewards benefit all of us.

## Allāh ﷻ: *The Best Judge*

One of the most important qualities of Allāh ﷻ is His Judgment. Allāh ﷻ is the best Judge and is Fair to everyone. His justice is always accurate. Allāh ﷻ wants all of us to be fair when we deal with others. Students will learn about Allāh's ﷻ judgment and why we should depend upon His judgment.

## What Does Allāh ﷻ Want Us to Do?

Allāh ﷻ commands us to perform all obligatory duties. In addition to these obligatory duties, Allāh ﷻ advises us on many other actions that we should do and those that we should not do. Taking the right action makes us better people. The right actions are not complicated to perform. In this lesson, students will learn some of these recommended actions.

# Who Is Allāhﷻ?

**Objective of the Lesson:**

A common question in the minds of many people is, "Who is Allāhﷻ?" We cannot see Him, therefore, how do we learn about Him? We learn about Him by learning some of His qualities. Allāhﷻ has given us a lot of information about Himself—His actions, His signs, His likes, and His dislikes. We also learn about Him by understanding our relationship with Him. When we learn all this information, we learn about Him.

If we want to know something about a person, there are several ways we can learn about the person. One way to learn about the person is to find out what he or she does. Maybe we would like to know what things he or she does not do. For example, if the person is a doctor, we might want to know at which hospital he or she works. Which area of medicine does the person specialize in—the heart, skin, bones, or another body part? If he or she specializes in the heart, can he or she work as a dentist? Can he or she repair a car, do landscaping, or work as an electrician? If the person does not work in a hospital, does he or she own a medical practice? Maybe the person simply teaches in a university. Maybe he or she is retired. We might want to know what language the person speaks. What is his or her

nationality? Does he or she have a family and children? We might want to know many other things to learn more about the person.

In the same way, if we want to know about Allāh﷾, we have to learn a lot about Him. Just saying that Allāh﷾ is our God and we worship Him is not enough. We can know Allāh﷾ by learning what He does and what He does not do. We can also know about Him by learning some of His attributes or qualities.

The fact is we cannot see Allāh﷾ because He is not like us. Therefore, in order to know Him, we have to learn what He says about Himself. In the Qur'ān, Allāh﷾ tells us many things about Himself. Let us learn some of the things that Allāh﷾ says about Himself.

## Allāh﷾ is One

The first and foremost thing about Allāh﷾ is that He is the One and Only. This means that in the entire universe, there is one Allāh—that is, one God. He, Himself, tells us there is no other god in this world or in the universe.

وَإِلَٰهُكُمْ إِلَٰهٌ وَاحِدٌ لَّا إِلَٰهَ إِلَّا هُوَ الرَّحْمَٰنُ الرَّحِيمُ ﴿١٦٣﴾

*And your God is the One God; there is no god but He, the most Gracious, the most Rewarding. (2:163)*

This message is repeated many times in the Qur'ān. The reason for repeating this is simple—so that people know that God is One and there is no other god. Therefore, people should never worship other gods.

## Allāh﷾ is the Rabb

The second-most important thing about Allāh﷾ is that He is the **Rabb**. In English, sometimes Rabb is simply translated as "the **Lord**." But the meaning of the word is much deeper. It indicates that Allāh﷾ has the power and ability to do many things.

Consider the example of the doctor. That doctor works as a physician; but he or she does not do plumbing, manufacturing, policing, or any other jobs. There is nothing wrong with the doctor because he or she specialized to be a doctor, not something else. On the other hand, the Rabb can do many things that human beings cannot do. First of all, the Rabb is the owner of everything on the earth and in the sky. He is the Rabb of all the worlds. In Arabic, we say He is the

رَبِّ ٱلۡعَٰلَمِينَ

**Rabbul 'Alamīn**

It means: Rabb of all the worlds.

Allāhﷻ is the Rabb because He created everything on the earth and in the universe. It is not possible that He would create and not take care of His creation. Therefore, He maintains, nourishes, provides, regulates, directs, and does many other things on the earth and in the universe.

## Allāhﷻ has no family

A family is a group of people, usually parents and children, living together in a household. We all begin our lives with a family. Animals, birds, fishes, reptiles, and most other organisms begin with some form of family. No living species can exist without some form of family. Having a family might make us feel complete.

This is not the case for Allāhﷻ. Allāhﷻ is the One and Only, so He does not need a family. Not having a family is not an indication of

incompleteness for Him. He does not have parents, nor does He have children. Before Islam, people in Arabia used to say the angels were the daughters of Allāh. Greek and Hindu mythology says their gods have wives and children. Christianity teaches that Allāh has a son. In the Qur'ān, Allāh declares that He has no daughters or sons.

## Allāh does not have a body

Now that we know Allāh is the Rabb of all the worlds, we might want to know what He looks like. Human beings have bodies with hands, legs, eyes, a nose, ears, and other body parts. Animals have different body parts. All plants have branches, leaves, and flowers as their body parts.

Allāh does not have a body like us. In the Qur'ān, He says that He "sees" us and that everything is in His "grip." This does not mean that He has eyes like us or fingers that grip as we do. These words are used only to help us understand. Allāh says:

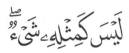

**Laisa ka-mislihi shaiun**

*Nothing is there in His likeness. (42:11)*

This means that we cannot liken Allāhﷻ to anything we know. Whatever form, shape, or image we think of, Allāhﷻ does not match up with our imagination. People who make images of God or who worship these images are participating in make-believe. These images are not God. We should remember that Allāhﷻ is not a man. Allāhﷻ is not a woman. We do not know how what Allāhﷻ looks like.

What is the meaning of Rabbul 'Alamīn?

_____

Write two things that Allāhﷻ does not have but we have.

_____      _____

## Where was Allāhﷻ?

Take a look at the sky during the daytime. You will see the blue sky and the bright sun, or you will see clouds. If you look at the night sky, you will see hundreds of stars. You will also probably see the moon.

You might ask, "Where was Allāhﷻ before the earth, planets, and sky were created?"

The answer is Allāhﷻ was always there. Long before the earth and the sky were created Allāhﷻ was there. Long after the earth and the sky are destroyed, Allāhﷻ will still be there. For this reason, we say Allāhﷻ is the **First** and He is also the **Last**. This means Allāhﷻ has no beginning, and He has no end.

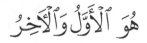

**Hua-l Awwalu wal-Ākhiru**

It means: He is the First and the Last.

## Allāh ﷻ is Eternal

The earth is about five billion years old. The Blue Ridge Mountains in the U.S., also known as the Appalachians, are believed to be 1.2 billion years old. Some animals, like the tortoise and the whale, can live for hundreds of years. Some trees are several thousand years old. For example, some Redwood trees in California are about 5,000 years old. Some Banyan trees in Hawaii and India are more than 500 years old. No matter how long they survive, one day they all will perish.[55:26] In comparison, there is no end to Allāh ﷻ. He remains because He is eternal—ever-Existing.

## Allāh ﷻ is free of all needs

All living things need something to survive. For example, human beings need air, water, and food to survive. Even non-living things need something to remain in existence. For example, a river needs a source of water to continue flowing. If the source of water dries up, the river will die. If a region does not get enough rainfall year after year, the area will become dry and barren. Allāh ﷻ does not need anything to remain

for eternity. He is free of all needs and wants. He is not dependent on anything, but everything is dependent upon Him.

## Allāh﷾ has beautiful names

Allāh﷾ has many beautiful names. These names are known as **Asma al-husna**. Nobody else has so many beautiful names.

$$ ٱللَّهُ لَآ إِلَٰهَ إِلَّا هُوَ لَهُ ٱلۡأَسۡمَآءُ ٱلۡحُسۡنَىٰ ۝ $$

*Allāh—there is no deity but He. To Him belong all the most beautiful names. (20:8)*

These names are Allāh's﷾ attributes or qualities. From these names, we learn that He is the most-Merciful, most-Rewarding, the Judge of the universe, and the Master of the Day of Judgment. His power is enormous. He is the originator, protector, and provider. He is most wise. He is aware of everything, everywhere. Nothing can hide from Him. He sees, hears, and knows everything. He knows about every leaf that falls from the tree. Think about this: every year, billions of leaves from millions of trees fall on the ground. Allāh﷾ knows about each one of them. His knowledge is perfect. He is watchful over everything. He is loving and generous.

## Allāh ﷻ does not sleep

All living beings must rest. Most animals sleep at night. Some animals sleep during the day and hunt at night. The main reason for sleep is to rest and regain energy. Human beings also need to sleep to rest. If we do not sleep for a long time, we will become very confused. After a good night's sleep, we wake up feeling refreshed. Some people take a nap during the daytime. Daytime naps help people regain energy.

However, Allāh ﷻ does not sleep or take a nap. He does not get tired, so He does not need to rest. Not taking a nap and not sleeping indicates that Allāh ﷻ is always looking after us.

$$ لَا تَأْخُذُهُۥ سِنَةٌ وَلَا نَوْمٌ $$

*...slumber does not overtake Him nor sleep... (2:255)*

What is the meaning of Hua-l Awwalu wal-Akhiru?

_____

Write three things that living things need to survive.

_____ _____ _____

## Master of the Day of Judgment

Islam teaches us that a day will come when everything on earth will perish. Then **Yaum al-Qiyamah**, or the Day of Awakening, will begin. This Day is known by several names. One of these names is the **Day of Judgment**. Allāh ﷻ is the Master of the Day of Judgment.

*Master of the Day of Judgment. (1:4)*

On the Day of Judgment, Allāhﷻ will judge every human being for their deeds. He will be the absolute Judge, and nobody will be able to change his ruling. His judgment will be accurate and fair.

This chapter presents only a short account of Allāhﷻ. Volumes could be written about Him, but we could never finish learning about Allāhﷻ. We should attempt to continue learning more about Him. The next few chapters will describe other aspects and attributes of Allāhﷻ.

## from Hadīth

Jabir bin 'Abdullāh reported that Nabi Muhammadﷺ said: "O Allāh, to You I have prostrated and in You I have believed and to You I have submitted, and You are my Rabb. My face has prostrated to the One Who created it and formed it and brought forth its hearing and sight. Blessed be Allāh the best of Creators."

1. Write four things about Allāh that you learned from the lesson.

| | |
|---|---|
| | |
| | |

2. What is the meaning of Rabbul ʻAlamīn?

_____

3. Write four things that Allāh—the Rabb—provides for His creations.

| | |
|---|---|
| | |
| | |

4. Circle **T** if the sentence is true. Circle **F** if the sentence is false.

| | | |
|---|---|---|
| We can see Allāh because He is like us. | T | F |
| Allāh does not have a family. | T | F |
| Allāh has a body like us. | T | F |
| Allāh is the First and the Last. | T | F |
| Allāh does not need anything to exist. | T | F |

5. Which of the following sentences is true?

    A. Allāh declares that He has one son.

    B. Allāh says that everything is in his grip.

    C. Allāh has a few beautiful names.

    D. After a long day of work, Allāh takes a nap.

6. What will happen on Yaum al-Qiyamah?

    A. Everything on earth will shine.

    B. All the deeds of human beings will vanish.

    C. Allāh will judge only the Muslims.

    D. Everything on earth will end.

7. Unscramble the following letters to make meaningful words.

**BRBA**    ☐☐☐☐

**PELES**    ☐☐☐☐☐

**EON**    ☐☐☐

8. What is the meaning of Asma al-Husna?

_____

# What Allāh﷾ Is and Is Not

**Objective of the Lesson:**

If everyone in the world fully understood what Allāh﷾ is and is not, then everyone would probably become Muslim. A large number of people in the world do not know much about Allāh﷾, therefore, they make images of God and worship these images. We do not need to imagine anything about Allāh﷾. We simply want to learn about Him from the information He provided in the Qur'ān. This lesson provides the important information we should know.

The most important and central point of Islam is teaching the oneness of Allāh﷾. As Muslims, we do not express doubt about the oneness of Allāh﷾. This is because Allāh﷾ Himself tells us that He is the one and the only—there is no god but Him. He does not have partners. We believe in this declaration. Allāh﷾ says:

*And your God is the One God; there is no god but Him, the most Gracious, the most Rewarding. (2:163)*

Sometimes, we might wonder what Allāh﷾ is and what He is not. The reason we wonder this is probably because we cannot "see" Him. There is nothing strange or silly about wondering about Him. Actually, it is a very important idea. If everyone in the world fully understood what Allāh﷾ is and what He is not, then everyone probably would become Muslim. But a large number of people in the world do not know much about Allāh﷾, or God. They have various ideas and beliefs about God. They might imagine that a God has a beard and looks like a man. Some think He has several hands and three eyes—these hands or eyes can shoot powerful fire to burn things. Some think God is like an animal—for example, a cow, dragon, eagle, elephant, monkey, owl, turtle, or snake. All of these ideas are wrong.

## Not easy to know

As you can see, it is not easy to know what Allāh﷾ is and what He is not. We do not need to imagine anything about Allāh﷾. We simply want to learn about Him from the information He has provided in the Qur'ān. In the past, people made images of God and worshipped these images. They were under the impression that they were actually worshipping God. Even today, many people worship images or idols. Allāh﷾ has not given us permission to make His image or to worship idols.

## No image or body

Whether God has a particular image or body has puzzled people for centuries. Even among Muslims, many people are unsure about it. In fact, there are Islamic writings that suggest Allāh﷾ has two feet, and that He sits on a pedestal when He needs to rest. These writings are false and have no value. Allāh﷾ does not have a specific body, nor does He have a measurable shape or dimension. He is not divisible, and He cannot be represented in bodily forms. He does not have the form of a cow, owl, elephant, dragon, or any other object as portrayed in some religions.

In the Qur'ān, Allāh﷾ mentions His "hand" and "grip," and that He "sees" and "hears." He even uses the masculine pronouns "He," "Him," or "His" when He refers to Himself. We should understand that Allāh﷾ is not a male or a female. If Allāh﷾ had referred to Himself as "it," this would mean He is an object or a thing. When we say "It is a table" we mean it is a lifeless object. A table has no mercy, kindness, or knowledge. A table cannot create, provide, sustain, judge, or forgive. If Allāh﷾ had used a feminine pronoun, it would indicate that Allāh﷾ is female. In order to avoid confusion, Allāh﷾ uses the masculine pronoun—not to suggest He is male, but simply to communicate with us. There is no maleness or femaleness associated with Allāh﷾.

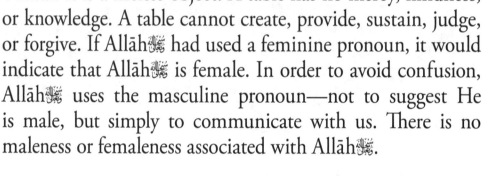

Regarding His "hand" or "grip," we should understand that these words are used to indicate His power and authority. On the Day of Judgment, the world will be in His grip, and the Heavens will be rolled up in His right hand. Such statements indicate Allāh's﷾ supreme power and authority.

### Allāh ﷾ is Sovereign

The word sovereign means "a supreme ruler" or "one who has supreme or ultimate power." Allāh﷾ says that He is **al-Malik**, meaning King or Sovereign, and **al-Malik-ul-Mulk**, meaning the Master of all worlds—here and anywhere in the universe—whether these worlds are known on unknown. He rules and regulates everything in the universe. He does all this by Himself, without the help of any partner.

So, how big is the universe? We do not have the capacity to even understand its size. Earth is like a microscopic dot compared to the size of the universe. Our solar system consists of many planets that are part of our galaxy—the **Milky Way Galaxy**. When we look at the night sky, all the stars that we see are only a tiny fragment of our galaxy. There are an estimated 100 to 400 billion stars, such as the sun in our galaxy. There are about 100 billion planets such as earth in our galaxy. How many galaxies are there? Scientists say there are at least 100 billion galaxies. Now consider Allāh—He is the Sovereign of all the visible and invisible galaxies in the universe!

## Allāh is the forgiver

Allāh created human beings with weakness in them. Because of these weaknesses, sometimes human beings make mistakes and commit sins. Allāh knows this. Therefore, He has prepared a path to forgiveness. Whoever asks for Allāh's forgiveness, will be forgiven. He is the forgiver. Forgiveness is one of His beautiful attributes. He says:

*...Do not lose hope of the mercy of Allāh. Surely Allāh forgives the sins altogether. He, surely He, is the most Forgiving, most Rewarding. (39:53)*

## Allāh is close to everyone

You cannot meet your governor or president anytime you like. You need to make an appointment. If you want the governor or president to attend your birthday party, most likely the person will not attend. He or she is probably too busy. They do not have time for you, and they are not close to you. In contrast, Allāh is close to everyone. You do not need to contact a middleman or an agent to reach Allāh. He is available to everyone, at every moment. You do not need an appointment to "meet" with Allāh. During every salāt and du'a, you are close to Him, and He is close to you. Allāh says:

*And when My servants ask you about Me, "Lo! I am near indeed." I respond to the call of the caller when he calls Me... (2:186)*

## Allāh ﷻ is free of all needs

As human beings, we need many things in life to survive. We need material things; we need food; we need parents and family; we need air, water, rain, and sunlight; we need education—the list is long. In contrast, Allāhﷻ is free of all needs. He does not need anything that human beings need. Most importantly, Allāhﷻ does not need our money. When we spend money in the name of Allāhﷻ—for example, giving zakāt, giving to charity, or donating to our masjid—the money does not benefit Allāhﷻ. It benefits us.

In order to truly understand Allāhﷻ, it is worthwhile to also learn what Allāhﷻ is not. A better understanding of Allāhﷻ will help us worship our Creator with the proper respect and honor.

✓ Write something that Allāhﷻ does NOT have.

_____

Write something that human beings need but Allāhﷻ does not need.

_____

## Allāh ﷻ is not an Arab God

Although the Qur'ān was revealed in Arabic and Rasūlullāhﷺ was an Arab person, this does not mean Allāhﷻ is an Arab God. Allāhﷻ is the God of the entire universe and for all living beings. He is the God for Hindus, Christians, Jews, and all other groups of people. Whether people believe in Allāhﷻ or not, He is still everybody's God.

The word Allāh is an Arabic word meaning "the God." The Qur'ān uses it as God's proper name. Arab Christians refer to their God as Allāh and the Arabic Bible mentions God as Allāh. If the Qur'an had been sent in another language, then Allāh'sﷻ name would have been a term from that language. Allāhﷻ is not a regional god. He is the God of the entire universe. This statement is mentioned a number of times in the Qur'ān.

رَبِّ ٱلْعَٰلَمِينَ

**Rabbil 'ālamīn**

*Rabb of all the worlds*

## Allāh ﷻ is not vengeful

To take revenge means to take action to get even with someone by causing injury or harm to the person. When a person takes revenge, he or she acts blindly without much reason. The revenge-taker loses his or her good sense and acts irrationally. Allāh ﷻ does not take revenge in that sense. His punishment is not the same as taking revenge. He never tries to get even with people. He is merciful. He is willing to forgive people for their sins.

## Allāh ﷻ is not cruel

Cruelty means willfully causing pain or suffering for others without having any concern about how it might hurt them. Sometimes people are cruel to other people, and sometimes they are cruel to animals. Many rulers in the world were cruel and ruthless. They tortured and killed innocent people for no reason. Even today, many governments are cruel to their citizens and deny them basic rights.

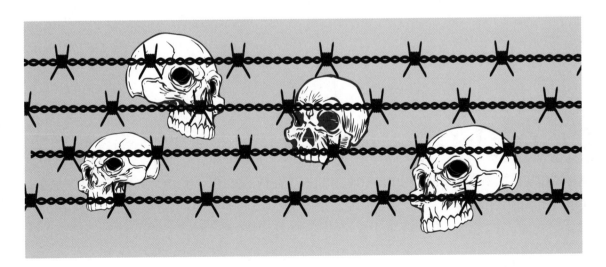

Allāh﷾ is not cruel to His creations. He is extremely merciful and compassionate. Allāh﷾ does not violate human rights. Even if someone commits a sin, Allāh﷾ does not punish the person immediately. He gives the person a chance to correct his or her mistake. He is ever-forgiving.

## God is not unjust, unfair or partial

As human beings, sometimes we are unfair to our friends or family. Sometimes we act in a partial manner—we favor someone and dislike someone else for no valid reason. Allāh﷾ is not unjust, unfair, or partial to anybody. We might think that Allāh﷾ is partial to Muslims and unfair to people of other faiths, but He is not. He treats everybody equally.

## from Hadīth

Anas ibn Malik reported that Nabi Muhammadﷺ said: "Every son of Adam commits sin and the best of those who repent."

1. Allāh﷾ is sovereign. What is the meaning of the word sovereign?

_____

2. Which of the following statements is true?

    A.  Some people know what Allāh﷾ looks like.

    B.  In the past, Allāh﷾ told people to worship idols.

    C.  Allāh﷾ is not a male or a female.

    D.  When we give zakāt, it benefits Allāh﷾.

3. Circle **T** if the sentence is true. Circle **F** if the sentence is false.

| | | |
|---|---|---|
| Allāh﷾ is an Arab God. | T | F |
| Allāh﷾ does not need anything except us. | T | F |
| Human beings have weaknesses in their nature. | T | F |
| Allāh﷾ is close only to Muslims, not to others. | T | F |

4. Unscramble the following letters to make meaningful words.

**ENEDS**

**LCSOE**

5. How many galaxies are there in the universe?

    A.  About 50 million.
    B.  About 100 million.
    C.  About 1,000 million.
    D.  About 100 billion.

6. In order to reach Allāhﷻ, which of the following is NOT needed?

    A.  A prayer.
    B.  Salāt.
    C.  A duā.
    D.  A middleman.

7. Which of the following sentences is true?

    A.  Allāhﷻ refers to Himself as "He" because he is male.
    B.  Idols are false gods.
    C.  The Heavens will not roll up in Allāh'sﷻ grip.
    D.  Malik-ul-Mulk means master of one planet.

# Allāh ﷻ: *The Most-Merciful, Most-Rewarding*

**Objective of the Lesson:**

One of Allāh's ﷻ most significant qualities is His mercy. Allāh's ﷻ mercy covers everything. Allāh ﷻ is also the most Rewarding. Does everybody receive rewards, or are there certain criteria to receive them? Students will learn why Allāh ﷻ is so merciful and how His mercy and rewards benefit all of us.

In a previous lesson, we learned that Allāh ﷻ has many beautiful names. These names are known as **Asma al-Husna**. Nobody else has so many beautiful names.

ٱللَّهُ لَآ إِلَٰهَ إِلَّا هُوَّ لَهُ ٱلْأَسْمَآءُ ٱلْحُسْنَىٰ ۝

*Allāh—there is no deity but He. To Him belong all the most beautiful names. (20:8)*

In another verse, Allāh ﷻ tells us to call upon Him using these beautiful names. To "call upon" means to ask, to request, or to cry upon. We call upon Allāh ﷻ during our prayers.

*To Allāh belong all the finest Names, so call upon Him by these...* *(7:180)*

## Ar-Rahman and Ar-Rahim

When we look at the list of Allāh's beautiful names, two names stand out the most. One of these names is **Ar-Rahman**, and the other is **Ar-Rahim**. These two names have a very similar meaning because they originate from the same root word. The name Ar-Rahman means "the most-Kind" or "the most-Merciful." This name tells us that Allāh is full of mercy and kindness towards everything. The name Ar-Rahim means "the most-Rewarding."

Ar-Rahman              Ar-Rahim

## Limitless mercy

Allāh says He covers everything with mercy. His mercy is limitless. Everybody and everything in the world receives Allāh's mercy. We do not have to do anything to receive His mercy. He simply gives us His mercy. It is like a free gift for each one of us. Allāh says:

*Say as to Allāh—He has prescribed Mercy on Himself. (6:12)*

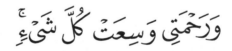

*But My Mercy extends to all things. (7:156)*

## Examples of Allāh's Mercy

Allāh has taken mercy upon Himself. This means He is full of mercy. His mercy extends to all things. Almost everything we see around us is an example of Allāh's mercy. The air, water, weather, plants, grass, trees, daylight, night-time—all of these are is an example of His mercy. Can you imagine what would happen to us without fresh air? Can you imagine what would happen to us if there were no daylight, no night, no water, no plants, no animals, no sun, and no food?

Allāh﷾ sends rain as a mercy for us. Can you imagine what would happen if there was no rain? The earth would become a desert, and all plants and animals would die.

## His Mercy is a gift

Allāh﷾ is so kind that He gives us many things as gifts. We do not have to do anything to earn these gifts. He gives these gifts on His own without anybody asking for them. Even if we sin, Allāh﷾ still gives these things to us. All these things existed even before we were born. Some of these things are the sun, the moon, air, water, plants, night-time to sleep, and day-time to work. His Mercy is a gift.

## Hadīth on mercy

In a hadīth, we learn that the Rasūlullāhﷺ said, "Allāh﷾ has divided Mercy into 100 parts, He kept 99 parts with Him and sent down one part to the earth, and because of that single part, His creatures are merciful to each other."

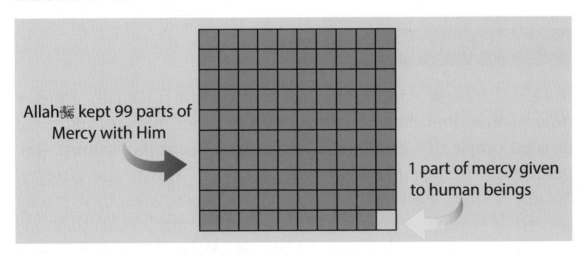

Allah﷾ kept 99 parts of Mercy with Him

1 part of mercy given to human beings

## Guidance is a mercy

Allāh﷾ is so Kind that He sends us guidance. Guidance is like a roadmap that tells us which way to go. If we did not have guidance, then we would be lost. Allāhﷻ sent guidance to all the people in the past. He sent nabis and rasūls to teach people how to become good people.

## Mercy to mankind

Allāhﷻ sent Nabi Muhammadﷺ as a mercy to **mankind**.

*And We have not sent you but as a mercy for all the worlds. (21:107)*

Nabi Muhammadﷺ taught people about Allāh'sﷻ message. Allāh'sﷻ message is written in the Qur'ān. The Qur'ān can guide everybody toward the Right Path. Therefore, the Qur'ān is a mercy for all people.[10:57]

Write three things that Allāhﷻ sent as a mercy to mankind.

_____     _____     _____

How many things does Allāh'sﷻ mercy reach?

_____

How many parts of mercy did Allāhﷻ keep with him?

_____

## Punishment can be mercy

If we sin, Allāhﷻ punishes us. The punishment is actually a mercy from Allāhﷻ. Punishment is meant to correct our mistakes and make us good people. If we commit one sin, there is one punishment. The punishment is never more than the actual sin. This is also a mercy, because Allāhﷻ does not give us ten punishments when there is only one sin. If we do one good deed, the reward is much more than one good deed. This is also because of Allāh'sﷻ mercy. He wants to give us more rewards than the good things we do.

Allāhﷻ is so kind that He does not punish us the moment we sin. He gives us enough time to realize our sins and seek **forgiveness**. If we promise never to commit the same sin again, then Allāhﷻ will forgive the sin. He might forgive almost any sin if we do not repeat the same sin. Allāh forgives because He is full of mercy.

## Ar-Rahim—the most-Rewarding

As mentioned previously, **Ar-Rahim** means Allāh is most-Rewarding. Let us understand the difference between the names ar-Rahman and ar-Rahim. As ar-Rahman, Allāh shows mercy to everything and everyone. As ar-Rahim, Allāh gives rewards to those who **earn** them.

Let us use an example. In your class, the teacher loves every student. Even if a student arrives late or does something bad, the teacher loves all the students. It is like Ar-Rahman—everybody is equal in receiving love and mercy.

What about a good student in the class? What about the student who finished all the homework and memorized a surah? This student should receive a reward. When the teacher rewards this student, it is like ar-Rahim—the reward is given only to those who earn it.

## Many rewards from Allāh

When a teacher gives a reward in class, he or she can give it to only one or two students. This is because the teacher only has a few rewards to give. In playing sports, only one person or team can come in the first place. Others come second, third, and fourth. Not everyone cannot be in the first place.

In the case of Allāh there are plenty of rewards. Allāh does not run out of rewards. Therefore, if all of us earn rewards, Allāh will give them to us. Allāh's rewards are the best.

1. Circle **T** if the sentence is true. Circle **F** if the sentence is false.

    Allāh's mercy covers everything.                                              T      F

    Nabi Muhammad was sent as a mercy for mankind.                               T      F

    When Allāh created mercy, He gave away 99 parts of                           T      F
    mercy and kept only one.

    Allāh gives a person ten punishments for one sin.                            T      F

2. Write three things that tell us rainfall is a mercy of Allāh. Your answer
   should show how rainfall benefits people.

    1. _____

    2. _____

    3. _____

3. Name four things that Allāh sent as a mercy for everyone.

    1. _____

    2. _____

    3. _____

    4. _____

4. Why is Allāh's punishment also a mercy?

    _____

5. What did Allāhﷻ send as a mercy to all the people?

_____

6. How many punishments will a person receive for committing one sin?

    A.  1 punishment.

    B.  5 punishments.

    C.  10 punishments.

    D.  Many punishments.

7. If you do one good deed, how many rewards would you expect to get?

    A.  1 reward.

    B.  5 rewards.

    C.  10 rewards.

    D.  Many rewards.

8. After a person commits a sin, when does Allāhﷻ punish him or her?

_____

9. Where is it mentioned that Allāhﷻ kept 99% of mercy with Him, and gave 1% to mankind?

    A.  In the Qur'ān.

    B.  In a hadīth.

    C.  In a poem.

    D.  In old books.

# Allāh ﷻ: *The Best Judge*

**Objective of the Lesson:**

One of the most important qualities of Allāh ﷻ is His Judgment. Allāh ﷻ is the best Judge and is Fair to everyone. His justice is always accurate. Allāh ﷻ wants all of us to be fair when we deal with others. Students will learn about Allāh's ﷻ judgment and why we should depend upon His judgment.

In a baseball game, there is an umpire. In a soccer game, there is a referee. There are referees in other games, too. Umpires and referees keep the game fair and make sure the players follow the rules. Umpires and referees see when someone breaks a rule, and they enforce the rules to keep the game fair. Players have to obey the decisions of the referee or umpire.

## Role of a judge

Similarly, in other areas of our lives, there are people who work like referees and umpires. They are judges. Judges listen to cases—people's complaints or lawsuits—and make a decision about who is right and who is wrong. Judges listen to both sides and issue a judgment that is fair. The place where judgments occur is the court. Some courts hear cases involving small lawsuits from the local area. Other courts hear cases involving lawsuits of the state or the entire country.

## Allāh﷾ is a judge

Allāh﷾ is also a judge. One of His most excellent names is **Al-Adl**, which means "The Just," because He is Fair to everyone. It also means one who corrects and sets matters straight in a fair manner. He has another name, **Al-Hakam**, which means "The Judge." It also means the one who is the only true judge, or the best judge. In addition, it means one who makes a final decision about all matters.

ٱلْعَدْلُ        ٱلْحَكَمُ

**Al-Adl**        **Al-Hakam**

## Allāh﷾ judges everybody

The two beautiful names mentioned above tell us that Allāh﷾ is the best judge and is fair to everyone. As the best judge, Allāh﷾ decides who is right and who is wrong. As a fair judge, Allāh﷾ judges all people in every state, and every country. Allāh﷾ judges every person from every religion.

## Justice is accurate

Before making a judgment, a human judge calls for **witnesses**. A witness is a person who saw an accident, crime, or other event and gives **evidence**. Evidence means proof. Evidence shows that an accident, crime, or other event occurred. A human judge will not know everything. The judge will make the decision based on the evidence he or she believes from the witnesses. Sometimes a witness hides evidence. In such cases, the judge cannot find proof that a person is guilty of doing something. As a result, a human judge might sometimes make a judgment that is not the best or that is not fair.

On the contrary, Allāh﷾ already knows all the evidence. He is the best witness. Even if someone hides evidence or if evidence gets damaged, Allāh﷾ knows about it. Nobody can hide evidence from Him.

*He knows what is in the heavens and on the earth; and He knows what you hide and what you disclose. And Allāh is Knower of what is inside the mind. (64:4)*

If a person hides evidence under a big rock, Allāh﷾ knows about it. Sometimes evidence might be so small that nobody cares. Sometimes evidence might be so old that nobody remembers. No matter what, Allāh﷾ knows everything about it.

*O my son! surely if there be the weight of a grain of mustard-seed, then be it inside a stone, or in the heavens, or in the earth, Allāh will bring it forth. Certainly Allāh is Subtle, Aware. (31:16)*

Sometimes, many people make a plan to give false evidence against someone. Long ago, there was a nabi named **Yusuf (A).** Several women gave false evidence against him. As a result, a judge sent Yusuf (A) to prison. The human judge did not know the truth. His justice was inaccurate. In comparison, Allāh's﷾ judgment is always **accurate.** Therefore, Allāh's﷾ judgment is the best and the most fair.

What are Allāh's two names that show He is the best judge?

_____     _____

What does a witness provide in a courtroom?

_____

What happens if evidence is false or is not provided in a courtroom?

_____

## Allāh will judge everyone

Most of the time, a human judge can make a judgment if someone brings a case to him or her. If nobody brings a case, justice will not take place. Sometimes a poor person does not have the means to file a complaint. In such cases, the poor person will not get justice. Sometimes a judge will not even agree to hear a case, so the person will not get justice.

Considering all these problems with our human justice system, we should remember that Allāh will judge everybody. Allāh will judge everyone, even if we do not complain to Him. A poor person will not be denied justice because he or she is poor. A rich person will not escape justice because he or she has money or power.

Allāh's judgment includes every action of a person—rich or poor—it does not matter. It is a total judgment.

## Forgiveness and judgment

Some people think that God is so kind that He will forgive all sins. But total forgiveness is not good. If a judge forgives everyone, the world will be full of sins. If Allāh forgives all sins, people will have no reason to stop doing bad things. If you do something good, you get a reward. This is the best judgment. If you do something bad, you get punished. If you do something bad and you are truly sorry, then Allāh might forgive you.

Allāh judges us on earth and He will judge us in the Hereafter. On earth, Allāh disciplines us—He rewards those who do good deeds and punishes those who do bad things. On earth, sometimes sinners are not fully punished, and sometimes good deeds are not fully rewarded. Therefore, Allāh will reward us or punish us on the Day of Judgment.

Our final judgment will be in the Hereafter. On the Day of Judgment, every human being from the time of Adam (A) will be judged. This judgment will be accurate and the most fair. If someone did not receive a full reward in this life, he or she will receive the best reward in the **Hereafter**. Similarly, if someone was not fully punished in this life, he or she will be punished in the Hereafter. Nobody can escape the judgment of Allāh.

Allāh is the best of all the judges.

أَلَيْسَ ٱللَّهُ بِأَحْكَمِ ٱلْحَٰكِمِينَ ٨

*Is not Allāh the Wisest among the judges? (95:8)*

## from Hadīth

Abdur Rahman bin Abu Bakr said, "My father wrote to 'Ubaidullah bin Abi Bakrah—who was the judge of Sijistan - saying: 'Do not pass judgment between two people when you are angry, for I heard the Messenger of Allāh say: No one should pass judgment between two people when he is angry"

1. Write two of Allāh's﷾ names that you learned in the lesson.

| | |
|---|---|
| | |

2. Mark with a ☑ if the sentence is correct. Mark with an ☒ if the sentence is wrong.

If some evidence is hidden under a rock, Allāh﷾ will not find it.  ☐

If you are sorry after doing something bad, Allāh﷾ might forgive you.  ☐

A human judge knows everything.  ☐

Allāh﷾ will judge every person from every religion.  ☐

3. Fill in the blanks using the correct words from the box below.

> **escape    reward    accurate    Hereafter    umpire**

An _____ is a judge for a game.

Nobody can _____ the judgment of Allāh﷾.

Our final judgment will be in the _____.

Allāh's﷾ judgment is always _____.

On the Day of Judgment, good people will receive a _____.

4. Find the following words in the word search puzzle:

> JUDGMENT    WITNESS    FAIR    PROOF
> COURT    ACTION

| | | | | | | | |
|---|---|---|---|---|---|---|---|
| D | C | H | L | A | W | O | C |
| A | L | M | F | A | I | R | O |
| E | R | U | Q | P | T | E | U |
| A | C | T | I | O | N | J | R |
| J | U | D | G | M | E | N | T |
| A | B | J | T | X | S | L | M |
| P | R | O | O | F | S | E | S |

5. What is true about Allāh's judgment? Circle the correct choice.

A. Allāh will only judge the animals.

B. Allāh is the best and the most fair judge.

C. Allāh will judge us in an unfair way.

D. Allāh will judge only the Muslims, not others.

6. In which two places will Allāh judge us?

A. On Earth and after we are in Heaven.

B. On Earth and in the grave.

C. On Earth and in the Hereafter.

D. On Earth and in the sky.

# What Does Allāh ﷾ Want Us to Do?

**Objective of the Lesson:**

Allāh ﷾ commands us to perform all obligatory duties. In addition to these obligatory duties, Allāh ﷾ advises us on many other actions that we should do and those that we should not do. Taking the right action makes us better people. The right actions are not complicated to perform. In this lesson, students will learn some of these recommended actions.

In Islam, some duties are compulsory for us. These compulsory duties are performing salāt, giving zakāt, fasting in the month of Ramadan, and performing Hajj at least once in our lifetime. These duties are part of the Five-Pillars of Islam that we learned in previous grades. If a person performs all these duties regularly, Allāh ﷾ will be happy and reward him or her.

In addition to these compulsory duties, Allāh ﷾ tells us many other actions that we should and should not do. Let us learn some of the actions that Allāh ﷾ recommends for us. The list of recommended actions is long, but the actions are not complicated. With a little practice, we can all perform these actions when we get the opportunity.

The most important message of Islam is to believe and admit that there is no god but Allāh ﷻ. In the Qur'ān, Allāh ﷻ asks us to worship only Him.

$$ وَقَضَىٰ رَبُّكَ أَلَّا تَعْبُدُوا إِلَّا إِيَّاهُ $$

*And your Rabb has commanded that you do not worship anyone except Him alone... (17:23)*

The best action we can take is to worship none but Allāh ﷻ. Not only does the Qur'ān teach this point again and again, but also our Nabi Muhammad ﷺ repeatedly taught us to worship only Allāh ﷻ. All past nabis and rasūls also taught the same message. For thousands of years, this has been the most important message for human beings.

### Respect parents

After worshipping Allāh ﷻ, the next important thing is to be good to our parents. Being good to our parents means not hurting them with

our actions or words. It is possible that sometimes we do not agree with our parents and do not want to hear their advice. Sometimes we think we know better and our parents do not understand us. No matter what we think, the Qur'ān reminds us that we should not be harsh to our parents. We should always respect them.

The Qur'ān tells us to treat our parents like a mother-bird treats her babies. It says we should lower our wings of mercy and compassion to our parents. When our parents become old, we should not speak to them in a disrespectful manner.

*...and do good to the parents. If one of them or both of them reach old age in your presence, even then do not say to them "Ugh", and do not scold them, and speak to them a generous speech. (17:23)*

## Be truthful

Allāhﷻ loves the truth because the truth is reality. Allāhﷻ teaches us to be truthful in our words and actions. We should not be afraid of the truth. Sometimes we think that speaking the truth will cause trouble, so we lie, thinking it will cause less trouble. Actually, lies cause more trouble. To cover up one lie, we often have to lie several times. Eventually, lies will be exposed. However, the truth is always appreciated. People love and respect a truthful person.

## Be good to relatives

Islam encourages us to have strong family relationships. The Qur'ān teaches us to be nice to our relatives. If our relatives have financial difficulties, we are required to help them. We should help them before offering help to others. As we learned, worshipping Allāhﷻ is our primary duty. After fulfilling this duty, we need to fulfill our duties to our parents. After that, our duty is to help our relatives.

## Be good to neighbors

Human beings are social by nature. We interact with friends, family, and neighbors. The Qur'ān and the teachings of Rasūlullāhﷺ encourage us to be nice to our neighbors. Our neighbors may not agree with us on everything. But we should be tolerant, forgiving, and kind to them. A hadīth mentions that Rasūlullāhﷺ said, "None of you have faith until you love for your neighbor what you love for yourself." (Sahih Muslim) Another hadīth reports that Rasūlullāhﷺ said, "None of you is a believer if he eats his fill while his neighbor has nothing." (Musnad)

## Be a good-hearted person

To be a good-hearted person means to behave in a kind, caring, generous, and well-behaved manner. You can be a good-hearted person if your mind is pure and you are sincere. A good-hearted person respects others. He or she will not argue, grumble, or speak ill of others. A good-hearted person will not be vengeful to others. He or she will not be cruel to people or animals. With a little practice, we can be kind-hearted people. Whenever you are in a situation that makes you angry, rude, or vengeful, ask yourself, "What would Allāh want me to do in this situation?" You will find your answer. Allāh wants you to behave in the right manner—to be a kind-hearted person. Allāh says:

*Your Rabb knows best what is in your minds. If you be righteous, He is then surely most Forgiving to those often turn [in repentance]. (17:25)*

## Be honest and truthful

The Qur'ān teaches us to be truthful in our words and actions. When you are truthful in your actions, you are being honest. Honesty means doing the right thing even if nobody is watching. If your actions are truthful, there is no reason to lie. It is forbidden to hide the truth when you know it. We should remember that half-truths are lies. Even a "white lie"—a harmless or trivial lie usually told to avoid hurting someone's feelings—is still a lie. If you are truthful and honest, then you are also a trustworthy person. Being trustworthy means someone can be relied upon to be honest and truthful.

## The best greetings

Allāh advises us to greet each other with the best greeting—the greeting of peace. When someone greets us by saying, "Assalamu Alaikum," we should respond with a better greeting or, at least, a similar one. A similar greeting would be, "Wa Alaikum Salam." A better greeting would be, "Wa Alaikum Salam, Wa Rahmatullahi Wa Barakatuh."

Why it is that one has to be truthful and also honest at the same time?

_____

What is the next best thing to do after worshipping Allāh?

_____

## Do not laugh at others

Sometimes people laugh at someone to make fun of the person or to make the person feel inferior. People do this to feel that they are better than the other person. Sometimes people bully a person for no other reason than they hate the person. Allāh﷾ tells us that we should not laugh at others because every person has something good and special about him or her. The person whom people laugh at might even be better than them.

## Do not use insulting names

Sometimes people use offensive or insulting nicknames to refer to a person. Maybe they use a mean nickname for fun or to make the person feel inferior. Making fun of a person's looks, weight, clothing, or behavior is not good. Allāh﷾ does not like it if we call people insulting names. Everybody should be treated with due respect and dignity. Allāh﷾ tells us:

*...and do not defame your own people nor call one another by nicknames... (49:11)*

## Do not cheat

The reason people cheat is to unfairly benefit or gain an advantage in a situation. Sometimes people cheat in a game or during an examination. Sometimes people cheat their government to get a benefit. The Qur'ān forbids us to cheat others. When we exchange something with someone,

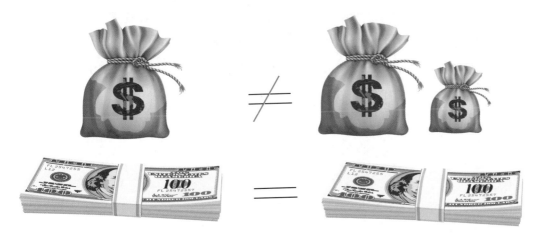

we should do it fairly way. We should not pay more and receive less, nor should we pay less and receive more without the knowledge of the other person.

## Do not listen to Shaitan

Allāh tells us that Shaitān is our worst enemy. Shaitān wants us to abandon our religion and get into trouble. Shaitān pretends to be our friend and suggests tempting ideas in our minds. If we listen to him, we will have problems. Allāh says Shaitān is an "open" enemy because Shaitān easily and openly tempts us to do bad things.

إِنَّ ٱلشَّيۡطَٰنَ لِلۡإِنسَٰنِ عَدُوّٞ مُّبِينٌ ٥

*Surely Shaitān is an open enemy to mankind. (12:5)*

## Do not waste

Everything we have is a gift from Allāh. Some of these gifts do not cost that much. Even if they cost a lot, we might not realize it. Allāh advises us not to waste anything. Whether it is food, water, clothes, or something else, we should not waste. Before eating, drinking, bathing, and so forth, we should remind ourselves not to waste.

*Eat and drink, and do not waste. Surely He [Allāh] does not love those who waste. (7:31)*

These are just a few of the actions that Allāh wants us to do and not do. Our lives will be much better if we follow these teachings. The teachings in the Qur'ān show us the right way to lead our lives. All the teachings in the Qur'ān are excellent and true. The Qur'ān does not have any false teachings.

1. Write four things that Allāh wants us to do.

|  |  |
|---|---|
|  |  |

2. When someone greets us, how should we respond?

_____

3. Mark the box with a ☑ if the sentence is true. Mark the box with a ☒ if the sentence is false.

Allāh wants us to respect our parents. ☐

The best action we can take is to worship Allāh. ☐

After worshipping Allāh, we should worship our parents. ☐

We do not need to be good to our relatives. ☐

4. Why should we not laugh at others?

_____

5. Which of the following sentences is true?

    A. The Qur'ān teaches us to be truthful in words, not in actions.

    B. It is fine to say half-truths, because they have some truth.

    C. Allāh﷾ knows best what is in someone's mind.

    D. It is fine to waste food because we can buy more.

6. Which of the following sentences about Shaitān is true?

    A. He wants us to keep our religion.

    B. He gives us good advice.

    C. He is our worst enemy.

    D. He is a secret friend of Muslims.

7. Find the following words in the word search puzzle below.

RESPECT   PARENTS   CHEAT   RELATIVES   SHAITAN
ENEMY   TRUTH   GREETINGS   LAUGH

| B | H | E | P | N | S | H | R | I |
|---|---|---|---|---|---|---|---|---|
| S | G | N | A | T | G | T | E | P |
| H | U | E | R | C | N | U | L | C |
| A | A | M | E | E | I | R | A | H |
| I | L | Y | N | P | T | T | T | E |
| T | C | C | T | S | E | E | I | A |
| A | X | J | S | E | E | H | V | T |
| N | D | N | R | R | R | D | E | G |
| I | D | X | N | S | G | Q | S | Q |

# Unit 2: Teachings of Islam

The objective of this unit is for students to learn some of the diverse and important aspects of Islam. Lesson 6 discusses the Arkan of Islam and the fundamental beliefs that make a person a true Muslim. Lessons 7 and 8 explain two of these beliefs in further detail. Believing in all the messengers proves that Islam is a religion for all of mankind. Lesson 9 touches on some of the features of hadīth and explains why they are important. Jinn are one of Allāh's creations. Lesson 10 discusses some of the features of Jinn. The teachings of Islam are universal, so its appeal spreads all over the world. Lesson 11 discusses the role of Islam and Muslims in North America. The final lesson in this unit explains the Straight Path—the path that Allāh wants us to follow. All these lessons attempt to provide a broad overview of Islam. The concepts discussed here will prepare students to learn about Islam in greater detail in future grades.

**Lesson 6:** **We Are Muslims:** *We Have 'Imān*

**Lesson 7:** **Belief in the Qur'ān**

**Lesson 8:** **Belief in the Messengers**

**Lesson 9:** **Hadīth and Sunnah**

**Lesson 10: Jinn**

**Lesson 11: Muslims in North America**

**Lesson 12: The Straight Path:** *The Right Path*

# Unit 2: Teachings of Islam

## We Are Muslims: *We Have 'Imān*

If we want to know someone, we need to know what he or she does and what he or she believes. What do Muslims believe? What do we do? The objective of this lesson is to explain our beliefs. These beliefs are the pillars of our faith. Students will learn about these pillars that make us Muslims.

## Belief in the Qur'ān

As Muslims, we believe in all the revealed books. The Qur'ān is the final revealed book. Muslims believe in the teachings of the Qur'ān and take them seriously in our lives. Students will learn many features of the last book. Understanding these features allows us to realize the majesty of the book and, in turn, makes us better Muslims.

## Belief in the Messengers

Belief in the messengers of Allāh﷾ is an important article of faith. All messengers have equal status. Muslims are instructed not to make any distinctions among the messengers. This lesson analyzes the article of faith about the messengers and explains the significance of upholding this belief.

## Hadīth and Sunnah

Two common terms in Islam are hadīth and sunnah. Students will learn about the similarities and differences between hadīth and sunnah. They will also learn about how hadīth were collected and about the famous collectors. Students will also learn what the Qur'ān says about following our Rasūlﷺ, whose saying are included in hadīth.

## Jinn

Jinn are one of Allāh's﷾ creatures. We cannot see them because they are invisible beings. Human beings and jinn have many similarities. Allāh﷾ created jinn for a reason. This reason is explained in the lesson. This lesson also summarizes some of the basic features of jinn.

## Muslims in North America

In this lesson, students will learn about Muslims in North America beginning from early settlement. Students will gain a basic understanding of where Muslims came from and when they arrived. This history reveals the challenges they faced and how they overcame these challenges.

## The Straight Path: *The Right Path*

The Qur'ān describes a Straight Path for living our lives. This Straight Path is the Right Path that Muslims should follow. Allāh﷾ loves the Right Path. He says we should always follow this Right Path. This lesson discusses the Right Path, how to tell which path is the right one, and how to follow the Right Path.

# We Are Muslims: *We Have 'Imān*

**Objective of the Lesson:**

If we want to know someone, we need to know what he or she does and what he or she believes. What do Muslims believe? What do we do? The objective of this lesson is to explain our beliefs. These beliefs are the pillars of our faith. Students will learn about these pillars that make us Muslims.

When we say we are Muslims, we should know why we are Muslims. What do Muslims do? What do we believe?

As Muslims, we must have certain beliefs. Our belief system is called **'Imān**. For example, we believe in Allāh as our God. This belief is an 'Imān. In Arabic, **'aqidah** means "belief." When people speak of Islamic 'aqidah, they generally mean Islamic belief. This belief system is vast and elaborate. But it is also very simple.

In addition to our belief in Allāh, we also believe in the angels and books of Allāh. These beliefs are also part of our 'Imān. As Muslims, we also have other beliefs. All of our 'Imān together makes a system of faith. This system of faith is Islam. People who follow Islam are Muslims.

## Arkān al-Imān

Let us learn a common Islamic phrase about our beliefs, **Arkān al-Imān**. The word **arkān** (اركان) means "pillars." Arkān al-Imān means "Pillars of Imān." These pillars are different than the "Five Pillars of Islam." The Five Pillars of Islam are about certain actions that Muslims take after they have Imān.

As Muslims, we have certain beliefs. These beliefs are the main parts of our 'Imān. There are **six** pillars of Imān. In order to make them easier to understand, sometimes they are broken down into seven arkān. These arkān are discussed below.

## Tawhīd

**Tawhīd** is about the belief that Allāh is the only God. This is the most important teaching of Islam. Due to this belief, Muslims never worship anyone or anything except Allāh. For the same reason, Muslims do not believe Allāh has any partners. The teachings of tawhīd tell us that He alone manages the entire universe. These teachings also tell us that nothing is equal to Allāh. He is the One and Only, therefore, He does not have a son or daughter. He does not have parents or a wife. He does not have junior gods or senior gods to assist Him.

## Belief in the angels

The second pillar of 'aqidah is belief in the angels. The Arabic term for angels is **malak** (ملك). They are invisible to us, but they can see us. We believe that angels exist and that Allāh created them. Angels follow Allāh's orders. They always glorify Allāh and ask Him for our forgiveness. There are no bad angels—all of them are good.

The Qur'ān mentions the names of several angels. The angels have different ranks and levels. The four most prominent angels are Jibril (A), Mikal (A), Israfil (A), and Malakul Maut, or the angel of death. Jibril

(A) brought the Qur'ān to Nabi Muhammadﷺ. The angels have many other duties. Some of these duties are to help the believers.

✓ What is the difference between Arkān al-Imān and the Five Pillars of Islam?

_____

_____

What is the meaning of Tawhid?

_____

## Belief in the books of Allāhﷻ

The third 'aqidah is belief in the books of Allāhﷻ. The reason we believe in the books is to acknowledge that Allāhﷻ guides us to be good people and to worship Him. His guidance is contained in the books that He sent to His chosen nabis. Before sending the Qur'ān to Nabi Muhammadﷺ, Allāhﷻ sent many other books to other nabis. Some of these books are the Tawrāt, Zabur, and Injīl. Suhuf, or short guidance, was sent to other nabis.

## Belief in the rasūls of Allāhﷻ

Rasūls are messengers who brought Allāh'sﷻ messages to people. We believe in all of Allāh'sﷻ rasūls. This is the fourth 'aqidah. The reason we believe in all the rasūls

اٰمَنْتُ بِاللّٰهِ وَمَلَائِكَتِهٖ وَكُتُبِهٖ وَرُسُلِهٖ وَالْيَوْمِ الْاٰخِرِ وَالْقَدْرِ خَيْرِهٖ وَشَرِّهٖ مِنَ اللّٰهِ تَعَالٰى وَالْبَعْثِ بَعْدَالْمَوْتِ

*Amantu billahi wa mala'ikatihi wa kutubihi wa rusulihi wal-yawmil-akhiri wal-qadri khayrihi wa sharrihi minallāhi ta 'ala wal-ba'thi ba'dal maut.*

I believe in Allāhﷻ, and His angels, and His books, and His Rasuls, and the Last Day, and in the measure—good or bad—is from Allāhﷻ, the Most High, and in the raising after death.

is because Allāh is the only God who guides all of humanity. In different time periods, only Allāh sent books to His chosen nabis and rasūls.

There are no differences among the rasūls. The rasūls were chosen to guide their people. Every community received its own messenger. Allāh sent the rasūls to different parts of the world. The names of all the messengers are not listed in the Qur'ān. Muhammad was the final rasūl of Allāh.

## Belief in the Last Day

The world will not last forever. There will be a **Last Day** for all creatures. We do not know the exact date of the Last Day, but as Muslims, we believe that the world and all its creatures will end on that day. We believe in **al-Akhirah**, or the Hereafter. This is the fifth pillar of 'aqidah. The fifth and seventh pillars are sometimes combined as one single pillar.

## Belief in Al-Qadr

The sixth pillar of our belief is **al-Qadr**. This means we believe that Allāh created everything in the universe and we believe He is in control of everything. He knows about every creation even before He creates them. For this reason, we believe that Allāh has prior knowledge of everything. Allāh knows everything good and bad that happens. He also decides what is good and what is bad. He measures everything for us.

Why is belief in the books of Allāh part of our Imān?

_____

Why is belief in the angels is part of our Imān?

_____

We believe that many things will happen during Al-Akhirah. One of our beliefs is that after the world ends, all the dead people will rise up. This is the seventh 'aqidah. The Day of Judgment will happen to reward those of us who were good and punish those who were bad. If we have faith and enough good deeds, then we will go to Heaven. Life in al-Akhirah will last forever.

We are Muslims because we have the same 'Imān. We might speak different languages, eat different foods, and wear different types of clothes, but we are all Muslims. We might be from different countries and different parts of the world. We might have different jobs and businesses, yet we are united. Our 'Imān binds us together.

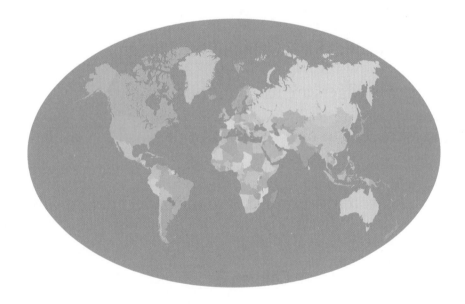

**from Hadīth**

Anas ibn Malik narrated that the most frequent du'a of Rasūlullāhﷺ was: "O Allāh! Give to us in the world that which is good and in the Hereafter that which is good, and save us from the torment of the Fire."

1. Write one sentence that describes the word 'Imān.

_____

2. Circle **T** if the sentence is true. Circle **F** if the sentence is false.

Tawhīd means to believe that Allāhﷻ is the only God.          T     F

Muslims do not have to believe in tawhīd.          T     F

The books of Allāhﷻ include the Tawrāt and the Qur'ān.          T     F

The names of all the messengers are listed in the Qur'ān.          T     F

All the messengers were sent to only one area of the world.          T     F

3. Draw a line to match the words in Column A to the correct definitions in Column B.

| Column A | Column B |
| --- | --- |
| Al-Akhirah | Belief |
| Tawhīd | Rasūl |
| Zabur | Hereafter |
| 'Imān | One Allāhﷻ |
| Messenger | Book of Allāhﷻ |

4. Write two things that will take place during Al-Akhirah.

    A. _____

    B. _____

5. Mark the box with a ☑ if the sentence is true. Mark the box with a ☒ if the sentence is false.

Allāhﷻ sent only two books to the prophets. ☐

Angels always follow Allāh'sﷻ orders. ☐

There are some differences among the messengers of Allāhﷻ. ☐

Tawrāt, Zabur, and Injīl are the names of some of the angels. ☐

There is nothing that can be equal to Allāhﷻ. ☐

6. How long will life last in al-Akhirat?

    _____

7. Which sentence is true about the names of the messengers in the Qur'ān?

    A. All of the names of the messengers are given in the Qur'ān.
    B. Only a few of the names of the messengers are given in the Qur'ān.
    C. Only 10 names of the messengers are given in the Qur'ān.
    D. Only 15 names of the messengers are given in the Qur'ān.

# Belief in the Qur'ān

**Objective of the Lesson:**

As Muslims, we believe in all the revealed books. The Qur'ān is the final revealed book. Muslims believe in the teachings of the Qur'ān and take them seriously in our lives. Students will learn many features of the last book. Understanding these features allows us to realize the majesty of the book and, in turn, makes us better Muslims.

In the previous chapter, we learned about **Arkān al-Imān**. Arkān al-Imān means "Pillars of Imān." There are **six** basic pillars of Imān. One of these pillars is belief in the books of Allāh﷾. There are many books of Allāh﷾—the final one is the Qur'ān. Before sending the Qur'ān to Nabi Muhammadﷺ, Allāh﷾ sent many other books to other nabis.

In addition to believing in all the revealed books, we are also required to believe in the final book, the Qur'ān. Allāh﷾ points out many features of the book. Understanding these features allows us to realize the majesty of the book, and, in turn, makes us better Muslims. The list of features is long, so we will focus on some of the most important ones in this chapter.

## A book of guidance

If someone asks us what is in the Qur'ān, one of the best answers would be, "It is a book of guidance." In the second verse of sūrah Baqarah, Allāh﷾ describes the Qur'ān in the following manner:

$$ذَٰلِكَ ٱلۡكِتَٰبُ لَا رَيۡبَ ۛ فِيهِ ۛ هُدٗى لِّلۡمُتَّقِينَ ﴿٢﴾$$

*This book, no doubt in it, is a guidance for the pious. (2:2)*

If we consider the Qur'ān a book of "guidance," it should contain complete guidance. If anything in it is incomplete or inaccurate, then it cannot be a true book of guidance. The Qur'ān contains the complete and perfect message of Islam, therefore, Allāh﷾ mentions the Qur'ān is a book of guidance many times. It guides us about how to lead a life in this world and gives us hope for a better life in the Hereafter.

Allāh﷾ also states the Qur'ān is a book of guidance for those who believe—that is, Muslims. But what about everyone else? The Qur'ān states it is a guidance for mankind—that is, everyone.

## Revealed in stages

The Qur'ān was revealed in short phases over a period of 23 years. In describing the process of revelation, the Qur'ān uses the term **tanzil**. The word means a slow and gradual process of sending something. Many verses in the Qur'ān were revealed in response to the questions people asked Nabi Muhammadﷺ. Many verses were revealed to address some critical social, economic, or political issues as they arose.

Part of the Qur'ān was revealed in Makkah. The rest was revealed in Madīnah.

## Easy to understand

As a book of guidance, the Qur'ān is easy to understand and follow. If the Qur'ān had complicated messages, then most people would not understand them. Even if some people understood the message, the meaning would be unclear to many people. Allāh made the Qur'ān easy to understand, and easy to read and memorize.

## Full of blessings

Many books can guide us in many different ways. For example, a travel book can guide us on traveling. A car repair manual can guide us on repairing a car. Can these books also bless us? No. The Qur'ān is a book of guidance and a book of blessings.

*A Book We have revealed to you abounds in blessings, that they may ponder over its verses, and that the possessors of understanding may reflect. (38:29)*

The Qur'ān is a book of blessings because its teachings provide so many benefits to our lives.

## A book of wisdom

The Qur'ān is also a book full of wisdom. Not all books can claim this feature. The most important thing is this wisdom comes directly from Allāh. Two of Allāh's beautiful names are **al-'Alīm** and **al-Hakīm**, meaning "the Knower of All" and "the Perfectly Wise," respectively. The Qur'ān was revealed by one who is Perfectly Wise, so there is no doubt that the Qur'ān is full of wisdom.

Many āyāt confirm the Qur'ān is a book full of wisdom. For example:

الَّرْ تِلْكَ ءَايَتُ ٱلْكِتَبِ ٱلْحَكِيمِ ۞

*Alif, Lam, Ra. These are the āyāt of the book, full of wisdom. (10:1)*

*These are the āyāt of the book of Wisdom. (31:2)*

*By the Qur'ān full of wisdom. (36:2)*

Wisdom provides us the ability to make good judgments about any matter. It helps us to gain understanding from the accounts of past people and past nations. We should remember that wisdom and knowledge are not the same. Many people have the knowledge, but they might not have wisdom. Knowing facts does not mean we will make good decisions. The best wisdom is to understand that God is One and to follow His teachings.

## For all mankind

There are many religions in the world. All religions have their own books of guidance for people to read. Some religions have several books, while others have one primary book. But none of these books are intended for all of mankind.

However, the Qur'ān is a book for all of mankind. Many of the teachings in the Qur'ān are directly addressed to Muslims, but overall, the message is for all of mankind. Allāh says:

*Surely We have revealed to you the Scripture for mankind with the truth... (39:41)*

## A source of healing and mercy

When you are hurt or sad, you want something that makes you feel better. Sometimes medicine makes you feel better. Sometimes, a kind word, friendship, or support can make you feel better. The Qur'ān contains many amazing teachings, and it is a source of healing and mercy for believers.

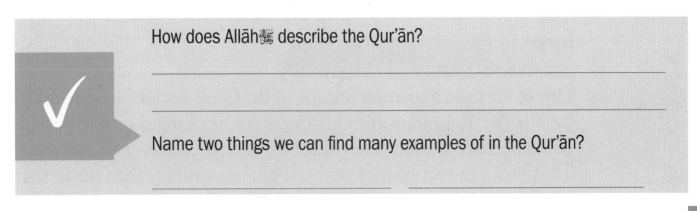

How does Allāh describe the Qur'ān?

_____

_____

Name two things we can find many examples of in the Qur'ān?

_____

If a person loses hope in life, or feels that his or her rights have been violated, or follows the wrong path in life, then he or she can find healing and mercy in the Qur'ān.

*And We are revealing out of the Qur'ān—that which is a Healing and a Mercy for the Believers; and it does not increase to the wrongdoers anything but loss. (17:82)*

## Mother of all books

The Qur'ān states that it is the "mother" of all books. A mother has a specific relationship with her children. She is the source from which children receive their nature. For example in the looks, behavior, or skills of a child, we can often see a reflection of the mother. Similarly, the Qur'ān is the mother of all religious books because many good teachings in these books are also found in the Qur'ān.

## Nobody could write another Qur'ān

When we believe in the Qur'ān, we also believe in its uniqueness. The Qur'ān is a book that cannot be imitated or re-written by anyone.

Everything in the Qur'ān is divine—it is from Allāh. Many authors and poets wrote brilliant works of literature. Many of these classics have been read by millions of people for hundreds of years. But nothing compares to the Qur'ān. In fact, the Qur'ān challenged people to compose one verse or one sūrah similar to one found in the Qur'ān. Some people attempted to write one, but nobody could do it successfully.

## Allāh preserves it

One of the most important features of the Qur'ān is how it is preserved by Allāh. This means the Qur'ān cannot be changed or modified by human beings. It cannot be ruined by natural or man-made disasters. The Qur'ān cannot be forgotten and become extinct. The Qur'ān that we read today is the same one revealed to Nabi Muhammadﷺ. Not a single word or letter has been changed since it was revealed over a thousand years ago.

Believe in the Qur'ān does not simply mean we believe it is a book from Allāh﷾. We also believe in its features, its uniqueness, and its promises.

from Hadīth

Anas ibn Malik narrated that the most frequent du'a of Rasūlullāhﷺ was: "O Allāh! Give to us in the world that which is good and in the Hereafter that which is good, and save us from the torment of the Fire."

1. What is the meaning of the word "tanzil?"

    A. Reading slowly.

    B. Sending something very quickly.

    C. Writing something carefully.

    D. A slow and gradual process of sending something.

2. Color the correct box. The Qur'ān is the _____ of all books.

| Mother | Father | Brother |
|--------|--------|---------|

3. Mark the box with a ☑ if the sentence is true. Mark the box with an ☒ if the sentence is false.

The Qur'ān is a book of guidance. ☐

The messages in the Qur'ān are easy to understand. ☐

People changed some of the words in the Qur'ān. ☐

The Qur'ān is only for Muslims, not for others. ☐

4. What challenges did the Qur'ān give to people that they could not meet?

    A. To memorize the Qur'ān in one month.

    B. To compose one verse or sūrah.

    C. To add 10 pages to the Qur'ān.

    D. To send copies of the Qur'ān to another country.

5. Which of the following sentences is true about the Qur'ān?

    A. It is a book of rhymes.

    B. It is a book for the Imām.

    C. It is a book of wisdom.

    D. It is a book of guidance only for Christians.

6. Which of the following sentences is true about the revelation of the Qur'ān?

    A. It was revealed over a period of 23 years.

    B. It was revealed to Muhammad ﷺ and then to Jibril (A).

    C. It was revealed only in Makkah.

    D. It was revealed as a completed book all at once.

7. Unscramble the following letters to make meaningful words?

| HREMTO | M | | | E | |
|---|---|---|---|---|---|

| CRYME | | R | | |
|---|---|---|---|---|

| OKBO | | | | |
|---|---|---|---|---|

# Belief in the Messengers

**Objective of the Lesson:**

Belief in the messengers of Allāh is an important article of faith. All messengers have equal status. Muslims are instructed not to make any distinctions among the messengers. This lesson analyzes the article of faith about the messengers and explains the significance of upholding this belief.

In a previous lesson, we learned that Muslims have certain beliefs or Imān. We have six important pillars of beliefs. These six pillars are the main articles of our Imān. One of our beliefs is belief in the messengers of Allāh. Our Nabi Muhammad was a messenger. Before him, there were many other messengers. Let us learn why belief in the messengers is one of the articles of our Imān.

## Islam is Allāh's religion

We know that Islam is Allāh's religion. We also know that Nabi Muhammad taught us the complete Islam. During Nabi Muhammad's time, thousands of people in Arabia became Muslim. Many more people became Muslims in the years that followed. But what about people who lived before Nabi Muhammad? Who guided them? Were they Muslims?

## Each community had a rasul

Before Nabi Muhammadﷺ, the world had a large number of nations and communities. These nations and communities had hundreds or thousands of people. Allāh﷾ regularly sent the message of Islam to people in different parts of the world. This means that Allāh﷾ also sent many nabis and rasūls to deliver these messages.

The nabis and rasūls taught their communities about Islam. They taught the most important message, which is:

لَا اِلٰهَ اِلَّا اللّٰه

**There is no god but Allāh**

## Not all messengers are mentioned

In previous grades, we read about some of the messengers. For example, some of these rasūls were Adam (A), Nūh (A), Ibrāhīm (A), Mūsā (A), and 'Isā (A). All of them lived before Nabi Muhammadﷺ. Some of them lived several hundred or thousands of years before Nabi Muhammadﷺ. Were all these nabis and rasūls the only messengers? No. The Qur'ān names many more messengers. However, the Qur'ān does not mention the names of many other messengers who were sent to other parts of the world.

Allāh﷾ made belief in all the messengers an article of faith because He wants us to know that Islam is not a regional religion. Islam is a world religion. Also, Allāh﷾ is not the God of only Arabs. He is the God of all mankind. He takes care of people wherever they live.

Based on the teachings of the Qur'ān, there were messengers in China, India, Africa, and other places. The Qur'ān does not mention all their names, so it is difficult to know who was a messenger in China, India, or other areas.

## Islam is not a new religion

The reason Allāh﷾ mentions that all past nations and communities received their own messengers is clear. It is to demonstrate that Islam is not a new religion established during Nabi Muhammad'sﷺ time. Islam is also not a regional religion or an Arab religion. It is a world religion.

## Make no distinction

To make a distinction means to make a difference. Allāh﷾ teaches us not to make any distinctions among the rasūls. We are not allowed to choose one messenger over another. A Muslim has to believe in all the messengers of Allāh﷾. Some of the rasūls and nabis are more famous than others because the Qur'ān narrates their lives in detail. Allāh﷾ might have even preferred one nabi or rasūl over another. But we do not have the option to reject or overlook one nabi or rasūl or prefer another.

## Messengers were human beings

Belief in the messengers also requires us to believe that they were human beings. Allāh﷾ did not send angels as His nabis to guide us. All nabis and rasūls were mortals.14:11 A mortal is a being that will eventually die.

What do mortals do every day? All mortals eat to survive and they also move around. The Qur'ān says that all the messengers ate food and walked around the markets.[25:20] The point is clear: they were human beings. Allāh🕮 gave all the messengers wives and children.[13:38]

Why does the Qur'ān point out this fact about the messengers? The reason is some people in the past demanded to receive an angel as a messenger. Only then would they believe. In response to their demand, Allāh🕮 made it clear that only human beings could be our messengers. Only human beings can be our role models, not angels.

## Messengers were not partners

One of the important teachings of the Qur'ān says that Allāh🕮 does not have any partners. Even angels are not His partners.

### He has no partners

It is very important to remember that none of the nabis or rasūls were partners with Allāh🕮. They were simply His servants. Therefore, Islam does not teach that the nabis or rasūls were divine, or god-like beings. None of them had god-like power. None of them told their communities to worship them.

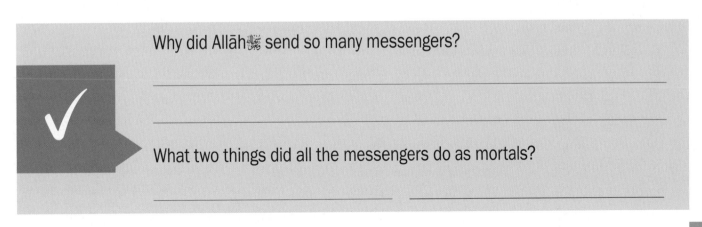

✔ Why did Allāh🕮 send so many messengers?

_____

_____

What two things did all the messengers do as mortals?

_____

## Messengers were truthful

All the messengers were truthful people. They always spoke the truth. In order to gain the trust of their people, the messengers did not lie or hid God's message. They were good people. They had strong determination. Even when they faced strong protests from their people, they did not become afraid.

## Messengers spoke local language

In order to speak to a community, a person must know the spoken language of the community. If a community speaks Hebrew or Arabic, there is no reason to send a messenger who speaks Spanish or Chinese. The people would not understand the messenger if he spoke a foreign language. For this reason, whenever Allāh﷾ wanted to send a messenger to a particular community, He chose a messenger from the same community.

## All messengers had enemies

The life of a messenger was not easy. All of the messengers faced many difficulties in their lives. All of them had enemies. People laughed at them. People said their messengers were liars, magicians, or crazy. But this did not stop the messengers from teaching the truth and speaking about Allāh﷾.

1. Mark the box with a ☑ if the sentence is true. Mark the box with an ☒ if the sentence if false.

Every community had a rasūl. ☐

The names of all the messengers are listed in the Qur'ān. ☐

Allāh﷾ is the God only for Arabs. ☐

Some messengers might have been Chinese. ☐

All of the messengers ate food and walked around the markets. ☐

2. How many messengers were mortals?

A.  10 messengers.
B.  Only Nabi Muhammadﷺ.
C.  About 15 messengers.
D.  All of the messengers were mortals.

3. Which of the following sentences about the messengers is true?

A.  Some of them were partners with Allāh﷾.
B.  Some of them had wives and children.
C.  They taught people to worship them.
D.  They taught "there is no god but Allāh﷾."

4. What does Allāh ﷻ say about making distinctions among the rasūls?

_____

5. Which of the following sentences about messengers is true?

    A.  All of them spoke Arabic.

    B.  All of them spoke the local language.

    C.  All of them knew how to read and write.

    D.  All of them wrote short sūrahs on their own.

6. Find the following words in the word search puzzle below. (search backward also)

RASUL   HUMAN   PARTNER   NATION
ISLAM   MORTAL

| L | U | S | A | R | U | S | M |
| N | R | N | O | I | T | A | N |
| K | E | L | F | U | M | E | U |
| H | N | M | O | R | T | A | L |
| U | T | C | N | S | N | H | E |
| M | R | M | A | L | S | I | T |
| A | A | L | P | V | S | T | S |
| N | P | N | P | L | U | B | J |

# Hadīth and Sunnah

**Objective of the Lesson:**

Two common terms in Islam are hadīth and sunnah. Students will learn about the similarities and differences between hadīth and sunnah. They will also learn about how hadīth were collected and about the famous collectors. Students will also learn what the Qur'ān says about following our Rasūlﷺ, whose saying are included in hadīth.

We all love our Nabi Muhammadﷺ. We cannot see him today because he lived over 1,400 years ago. During Nabi Muhammad'sﷺ time, thousands of people saw him. Many of those people tried to remember the words and actions of the Nabiﷺ. People observed how he reacted to a certain situation, how he solved a problem, or how he answered a question. His actions, statements, and responses influenced a large number of people. They fondly remembered these actions, statements, and responses.

After Islam spread to different countries, people in those countries also wanted to learn more about Nabi Muhammadﷺ. They wanted to know how he handled certain situations, how he solved a problem, or how answered a question. People who remembered these actions and responses told others about what they knew about Nabi Muhammad ﷺ. This was a new way of learning about Nabi Muhammad ﷺ.

## Hadīth and Sunnah

Two words that are very common in Islam are **hadīth** and **sunnah**. The words of Nabi Muhammad ﷺ are known as hadīth. Occasionally, a hadīth includes the words or actions of the Companion of Nabi Muhammad ﷺ. The word hadīth is singular, and **ahadīth** is plural. The books that contain the collections of ahadīth are also called hadīth.

The word sunnah means the **religious teachings** and **religious practices** of Nabi Muhammad ﷺ. When we say "sunnah of the Nabi ﷺ," we mean the behavior or conduct of the Nabi ﷺ. When we say hadīth, we mean the sayings of the Nabi ﷺ.

## The Qur'an on hadīth and sunnah

The Qur'ān tells us to obey Nabi Muhammad ﷺ and to follow his example of behavior and conduct. The reason we should follow him is explained beautifully in the following āyah. He is our role model—in him we find the best example.

$$ لَّقَدْ كَانَ لَكُمْ فِي رَسُولِ ٱللَّهِ أُسْوَةٌ حَسَنَةٌ لِّمَن كَانَ يَرْجُوا۟ ٱللَّهَ وَٱلْيَوْمَ ٱلْءَاخِرَ وَذَكَرَ ٱللَّهَ كَثِيرًا ۝ $$

*Certainly you have had in the Rasul of Allāh an excellent exemplar for him who is confident of Allāh and the Future day, and who remembers Allāh much. (33:21)*

In another āyah, Allāh ﷻ teaches us:

$$ وَأَطِيعُوا۟ ٱللَّهَ وَٱلرَّسُولَ لَعَلَّكُمْ تُرْحَمُونَ ۝ $$

*And obey Allāh and the Rasul that you may be shown mercy. (3:132)*

## Collection of hadīth

After Nabi Muhammadﷺ passed away, many people learned about the life of the Nabiﷺ through people who had seen him. After many years, the people who had seen the Nabiﷺ also passed away. People thought they would begin to forget the actions and sayings of the Nabiﷺ. So they began writing down what people remembered.

The collection of ahadith was long and difficult work. The few individuals who collected ahadith had to ask people who remembered the hadith. The collectors had to examine whether the hadith was true. They had to verify whether others knew about a particular hadith. If they did, how many people knew about it? If someone said they heard the hadith from their father, grandfather, or someone they knew, then the collectors verified whether those people actually knew about the hadith. The hadith collectors traveled throughout their countries and interviewed a large number of people. This is how ahadith were finally collected.

## Sahih Bukhārī

The most famous hadīth collector was **Imam Al-Bukhārī**. Bukhārī was born about 170 years after the Nabiﷺ. He lived in Iran. Bukhārī was very intelligent and had a good memory. He collected a large number of ahadith. He interviewed people to find out whether a hadith was true. He discarded the ones that he thought were not true or seemed strange.

Bukhārī wrote down the ahadith and classified them by topics. His book contains many chapters. He collected more than 7,000 ahadith. These ahadith are known as *Sahih,* or true. Imam Bukhārī's collection of hadith is the best-known collection.

## Sahih Muslim

Another learned person, named **Imam Muslim**, also collected many Sahih ahadith. He was also born in Iran. He lived several years after

Imam al-Bukhārī's time. Like Bukhārī, Imam Muslim also traveled widely to collect ahadith. He wrote many books, but the most important one is his collection (*Jami'*) of hadīth. His collection is known as **Sahih Muslim**.

### Other books of hadīth

Four other people also collected important ahadith and put them into books. Their names are **Abu Da'wud**, **Tirmidhi**, **an-Nasa'i**, and **Ibn Majah**.

These six books of ahadith are known as **As-Sahih As-Sitta**, or "the true six."

The six collectors of hadīth took great care to ensure that the hadīth came from reliable people. A reliable person is someone whom you can trust.

## Position of hadīth

The Qur'ān is the teachings of Allāh. The words in the Qur'ān are the words of Allāh. The hadīth are the words of the Nabi or the words of people describing the actions of the Nabi. The Qur'ān is the main source of Islamic teachings, while hadīth are the second source of religious teachings. Books of hadīth contain many good teachings about how to live our lives.

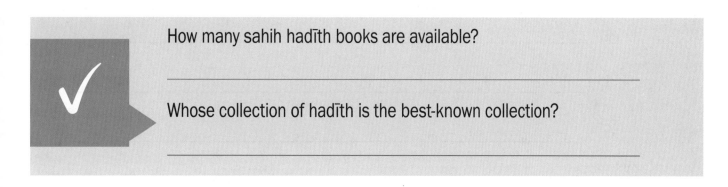

How many sahih hadīth books are available?

_____

Whose collection of hadīth is the best-known collection?

_____

1.  Write the names of the six collectors of hadīth.

    1. _____

    2. _____

    3. _____

    4. _____

    5. _____

    6. _____

2.  Circle the correct answer. Imam al-Bukhārī was born about:

    A.  7 years after the Nabiﷺ.

    B.  170 years after the Nabiﷺ.

    C.  500 years after the Nabiﷺ.

3.  Circle **T** if the sentence is true. Circle **F** if the sentence is false.

    Hadīth is the word of Allāh﷽.                          **T**    **F**

    As-Sahih As-Sitta is a collection of six hadīth books.    **T**    **F**

    Imam Muslim was born before Muhammadﷺ.             **T**    **F**

    The collections of Imam Bukhārī are Sahih Hadith.    **T**    **F**

4. How many people saw Nabi Muhammad ﷺ during his lifetime?

    A. 1,000 people.

    B. 10,000 people.

    C. 25,000 people.

    D. More than 25,000 people.


5. Which book records the words and actions of Nabi Muhammad ﷺ?

    A. The Qur'ān.

    B. Hadīth.

    C. Al-Sitta.

    D. Al-Furqan.


6. Circle **T** if the sentence is correct. Circle **F** if the sentence is false.

| | |
|---|---|
| When Bukhārī was a child, he met Nabi Muhammad ﷺ. | **T**   **F** |
| Nabi Muhammad ﷺ helped Imam Muslim write the hadīth. | **T**   **F** |
| Only four hadīth writers lived during Nabi Muhammad's ﷺ lifetime. | **T**   **F** |

# Jinn

**Objective of the Lesson:**

Jinn are one of Allāh's creatures. We cannot see them because they are invisible beings. Human beings and jinn have many similarities. Allāh created jinn for a reason. This reason is explained in the lesson. This lesson also summarizes some of the basic features of jinn.

We know that Allāh created everything in the universe. We also know that Allāh created the angels. Today, we will learn about another creation of Allāh. This creation is **Jinn**. They are creatures that remain hidden. Jinn are invisible to us, so we do not know their shape, size, form, or color.

Both the Qur'ān and hadīth describe how jinn were created. In the Qur'ān, Allāh says that jinn were created from a smokeless flame of fire.

*And the Jinn, We created them earlier from the fire of scorching wind. (15:27)*

In another verse, Allāh says:

*And He created the jinn from a smokeless flame of fire. (55:15)*

## Creation of Jinn

The jinn were created before human beings. Human beings were created from clay, and angels were created from light. Angels and jinn are different. Jinn are not bad angels because angels cannot be bad. Jinn were created from fire, so their nature is fiery. This means that sometimes they do not listen to commands—their nature is to protest, refuse, or deny. Some of them are also proud.

## Jinn and human beings

Human beings and jinn have many similarities. Jinn have some of the same qualities as human beings. For example, jinn are intelligent. They have the ability and freedom to choose between right and wrong. Therefore, some jinn are good and others are bad. The good jinn pray to Allāh.[72:14] The Qur'ān mentions that some jinn came to listen to the recitation of the Qur'ān. These jinn said:

*And some among us are the righteous, while some of us are not so. We are sects having different ways. (72:11)*

This means that jinn have divisions among them, and they have different religious beliefs. They can choose whether to worship Allāh. Just like some human beings, some jinn also disobey Allāh or do not believe in Him. However, angels do not have the freedom to choose. They always worship and obey Allāh.

Like humans, jinn are expected to worship Allāh and follow the right path. Their purpose in life is exactly the same as human beings. In the Qur'ān, Allāh says He created mankind and jinn to worship Him. If human beings disobey Allāh, they will face punishment. Similarly, jinn who disobey Allāh will also face punishment.

وَمَا خَلَقْتُ ٱلْجِنَّ وَٱلْإِنسَ إِلَّا لِيَعْبُدُونِ ﴿٥٦﴾

*I did not create the Jinn and mankind except to worship Me. (51:56)*

What two qualities do jinn and human beings have in common?

1. _____   2. _____

From what type of fire were jinn created?

_____

## Shaitan is a jinn

As mentioned previously, some jinn are bad while other jinn are good. The bad jinn do not pray to Allāh. They disobey Allāh and try to harm people. The jinn who disobey and do not believe in Allāh are called **Shayatin**. They tell people lies and make fools of them. They tell people to abandon Islam. Because of this, Allāh says He will send many bad jinn and men to Hell.

*And the word of your Rabb has been fulfilled: "Surely I shall fill Hell with jinn and mankind altogether." (11:119)*

Iblis is a bad jinn. He is also called Shaitān because he is evil. He is very proud. Iblis refused to obey Allāh's orders. When Allāh created Adam (A), all the angels submitted to human beings. Iblis refused to submit to humans.[18:50] He thought he was better than humans, and Allāh condemned Iblis. Iblis asked Allāh to give him the opportunity to confuse people and lead them astray. However, Shaitān cannot confuse or lead astray the true believers.

## Rasuls among jinn

We know that Allāh sent rasūls, or messengers, to guide human beings. These rasuls were human beings. Allāh also sent rasūls to jinn community.[6:130] These messengers told jinn about Allāh and warned them about the Day of Judgment. The good jinn listened to the messengers, but the bad jinn only wanted to have a good time and did not listen.

One time some good jinn visited Nabi Muhammadﷺ and listened to the recitation of the Qur'ān. This incident is mentioned twice in the Qur'ān.[46:29; 72:1] The jinn liked the recitation so much, they became Muslims. Then these Muslim jinn asked their friends and families to become Muslims.[46:30]

*And remember! We turned towards you a company of jinn who listened to the Qur'ān; so that when they appeared to it, they said: "Be silent!" And when it was finished, they returned to their people becoming warners. (46:29)*

*They said: "O our people! surely we have heard a scripture, sent after Mūsā, confirming what was before it, guiding towards the Truth and towards the right way. (46:30)*

*"O our people! respond to the Inviter to Allāh, and believe in Him He may forgive you some of your sins, and He may protect you from a painful punishment." (46:31)*

## Powers and abilities of jinn

Jinn have special power and abilities. Some jinn are useful to human beings. Sulaimān (A) had many jinn who worked for him.[34:12] They built his palaces and dove into the sea to retrieve pearls. Sulaimān (A) ruled a very rich country, and the jinn performed a lot of work for him.

## Jinn are not demons

People tell many different stories about jinn and haunted houses. But jinn are not demons or ghosts. Bad jinn do not try to scare us. They talk very nicely to us.[6:112] They use tempting words to mislead people.[6:128] They attempt to get people to do bad things. We would not do bad things if we were afraid of them. So the bad jinn and Shaitān always whisper nicely to us, using tempting words. They try to make us believe that bad things are good for us, and that good things are boring. We should be careful of jinn and people who give us bad advice.[114:6]

1. Write **T** if the sentence is true. Write **F** if the sentence is false.

A. ____ Jinn are always bad.

B. ____ Some good jinn visited Nabi Muhammadﷺ and listened to the recitation of the Qur'ān.

C. ____ Some jinn tell us to do bad things.

D. ____ Iblis was an angel.

2. Color the box that has the correct answer.

A. Jinn are made of      ( fire )    ( rocks )

B. A good jinn can be      ( a Muslim )    ( an angel )

C. Bad jinn talk in a      ( scary voice )    ( nice voice )

D. Good jinn worked for      ( Sulaiman (A) )    ( Pharaoh )

3. Write the name of one jinn that you learned about in the lesson.

_____

4. Mark the box with a ☑ if the sentence is true. Mark the box with an ☒ if the sentence if false.

Jinn have the ability to choose between right and wrong.    ☐

Jinn were created after human beings were created.    ☐

Allāh﷾ sent rasuls to the jinn to guide them.    ☐

5. Circle **T** if the sentence is correct. Circle **F** if the sentence is false.

| | | |
|---|---|---|
| Iblis was a jinn. | T | F |
| Human beings and jinn have some similarities. | T | F |
| Jinn were created from black mud and rocks. | T | F |
| The Qur'ān says that some jinn listened to the recitation of the Qur'ān and became Muslims. | T | F |
| We should listen to jinn because they guide us to the right path. | T | F |

6. What did Allāhﷻ use to create jinn?

   A. Smoky charcoal.

   B. Smokeless flame of fire.

   C. Clay and mud.

   D. Rocks.

7. Unscramble the following letters to make meaningful words.

   **URALS** ☐☐☐☐☐

   **IERF** ☐☐☐☐

# Muslims in North America

**Objective of the Lesson:**

In this lesson, students will learn about Muslims in North America beginning from early settlement. Students will gain a basic understanding of where Muslims came from and when they arrived. This history reveals the challenges they faced and how they overcame these challenges.

There are about 1.4 billion Muslims in the world. In North America alone, there are about eight million Muslims. About six million of them are in the U.S., and the rest are in Canada and Mexico. Most Muslims live in Asia and Africa. Compared to the total Muslim population in the world, only a small percentage live in North America.

Today, North American Muslims can be divided into three categories. In fact, Muslims in many other areas, including Australia and Europe, can be divided into three categories.

## The immigrants

The first category of Muslims in North America and in many other areas is **immigrant** Muslims. An immigrant is a person who was born in one country but moves to a different country. Muslim immigrants

are the largest category of Muslims in North America.

Most of the immigrant Muslims came to North America in the 80s, 90s, and thereafter. The government in North America is kind enough to allow immigrants from all faiths and countries to come and settle in this country. When a particular country faced a major disaster, North America allowed a large number of people from these countries to come and settle in this country. The majority of the immigrants come to North America on the basis of their education and qualification.

Now, each year, more than 1 million immigrants come to the USA every year. Of these 1 million, Muslims represent a small percentage.

## The second category

The second category is the Muslims are the ones who were born in a country where their parents came as immigrants. Many of you who are reading this lesson was born in North America.

## The reverts

The third category of Muslims is the **reverts**. These Muslims grew up practicing another religion, but then they accepted Islam. The reverts found true guidance in Islam. They abandoned the religion their parents and families practiced to become part of the large Islamic family.

## Better opportunity

Most immigrant Muslims moved to North America for better work opportunities and better educational opportunities. Many people moved to escape oppression and hardship in their home countries.

For example, large groups of immigrants came from Afghanistan, Bangladesh, Iraq, Somalia, Syria, and African countries.

Through their efforts, many people in North America accepted Islam. Most of the early reverts in the U.S. were African-American. Islam offered them respect, fair treatment, and equality, which many other religions did not provide. One famous African-American Muslim was **Malcolm X**. The heavyweight boxing champion **Muhammad Ali** was a Christian, but he accepted Islam later. Many Caucasian and Hispanic people also accepted Islam, and some of them even became leaders of Islam.

## Early history of immigrants

Many Muslims began to arrive in North America in the early 1900s. However, several hundreds of years before that, Muslims from Africa traveled to the Americas. When **Christopher Columbus** arrived in America, some of the members of his crew were Muslim sailors. Soon after Columbus arrived in America, Muslims from Spain and Portugal started traveling to North America. Some reports state that even before Columbus reached America, Muslim sailors helped many Spanish and Portuguese people travel to America.

Some reports state that long before Columbus, Muslim sailors from **North Africa** routinely traveled to America. They traveled from Morocco and other North African countries. At that time there were not many Muslim travelers. Their ships were small and only able-bodied males could go to America. Later on, some of them brought their families. By all accounts, survival in the New World was difficult for them and many others.

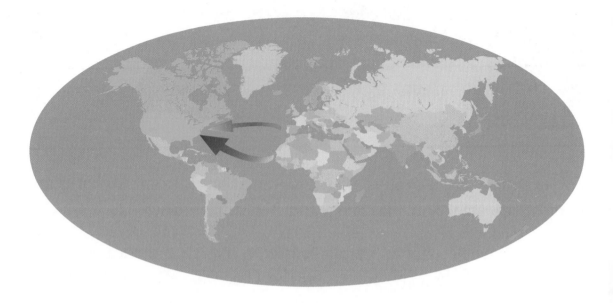

When Columbus traveled to America, he was surprised to find that many places had Arabic names. How did this happen? Muslim sailors traveled to America before Columbus and named these places. The Muslims who arrived during and after Columbus did not establish masajid. Even if they had, these masajid would not have remained for very long. Due to the strong influence of other religions, the early Muslims could not continue practicing their faith. After they died, their children abandoned Islam.

Hundreds of years earlier, large groups of people were forcefully brought to America against their will. They were brought here as slaves. Among these slaves, many were Muslim. Some of the Muslims were well-educated people and a few were from African royal families.

### Arrivals in the 1900s

Write the name of one North African country from which Muslims came to America.

_____

During Columbus's lifetime, Muslims came to America from which two European countries?

_____

In the early 1900s, Muslims from different countries again began arriving in North America. During this period large numbers of people from Europe immigrated to North America. Europe had suffered two World Wars. People fled their countries and moved to North America. They came to North America looking for better opportunities and better life.

Muslims who arrived in the 1900s made sure that masajid were established. These masajid or mosques gave Muslims an identity and helped them build an Islamic brotherhood. Today, wherever Muslims settle, they try to build masjid. Muslims also form schools to teach their children about Islam and the importance of following Allāh's teachings.

Picture of early slavery in the USA. Slaves were made to work in inhuman conditions and treated very badly.

1. In North America, most of the early revert Muslims were from which community?

_____

2. When did Muslim sailors routinely travel to North America?

_____

3. What did the early Muslims fail to do in North America during Columbus's lifetime?

_____

4. Circle **T** if the sentence is correct. Circle **F** if the sentence is false.

Muslims traveled to North America long before Columbus arrived.     **T     F**

Muslims began to arrive in North America only in 1990.     **T     F**

Malcolm X was a heavyweight boxing champion.     **T     F**

5. Mark the box with a ☑ if the sentence is true. Mark the box with an ☒ if the sentence is false.

During Columbus's lifetime, most Muslims traveled to North America from India.     ☐

The largest category of Muslims in North America is immigrants.     ☐

When people become Muslim, they earn fair treatment and equality.     ☐

Most of the early Muslims in North America were brought as slaves.     ☐

6. Find the following words in the word search puzzle:

COLUMBUS   AMERICA   SAILOR   SPAIN   REVERT
FREE   MOSQUE   MOROCCO

```
G  M  E  T  A  G  L  M
C  O  L  U  M  B  U  S
R  R  F  R  E  E  B  X
E  O  D  E  R  P  S  C
V  C  S  A  I  L  O  R
E  C  R  Y  C  V  K  L
R  O  S  P  A  I  N  Q
T  M  O  S  Q  U  E  F
```

WEEKEND 12 Classwork

# The Straight Path: *The Right Path*

**Objective of the Lesson:**

The Qur'ān describes a Straight Path for living our lives. This Straight Path is the Right Path that Muslims should follow. Allāhﷻ loves the Right Path. He says we should always follow this Right Path. This lesson discusses the Right Path, how to tell which path is the right one, and how to follow the Right Path.

In Islam, we often hear about the **Straight Path**. The straight path is mentioned sūrah Fātihah, in ayah 6. In Arabic, it is called **Sirātal Mustaqīm** (ٱلصِّرَٰطَ ٱلْمُسْتَقِيمَ). Here, the word "*sirāt*" means "path." The word "*mustaqīm*" means "straight," "smooth," or "shortest." In sūrah Fātihah, we pray to Allāhﷻ to guide us on the Straight Path.

ٱهْدِنَا ٱلصِّرَٰطَ ٱلْمُسْتَقِيمَ ۝٦

*Guide us on the Straight Path. (1:6)*

## What is the Straight Path?

The Straight Path is not a path of gravel, rocks or concrete on which we can walk, ride a bike, or drive a car. It is not an imaginary path, either. Nabi Muhammadﷺ followed this path. All the other past nabis and rasūls also followed the Straight Path. This is the path of all good Muslims. We should always follow this path. The Straight Path shows us how to live our lives. It is described as a "path" because it leads us to a good ending.

## Shortest path

One important feature of the straight path is that it is the shortest path between Point A and Point B. It is the direct path. If the path was curved or winding, then the distance between the two points would be longer.

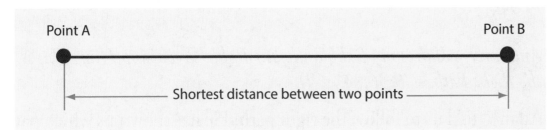

Allāh﷾ mentioned His chosen path as a "straight path" to point out that it is easy to follow on a straight path. A direct path is the best path to follow. Your view is not obstructed because you can see far in the distance. There is no danger on this path. The path is not curved or winding, so there are no unnecessary complexities on the path. There is no risk of ambush because there are no curves where danger might lurk. If we choose this path, it is less likely that we will wander away. The word *mustaqīm* also means "smooth." Thus, the straight path is comfortable and easy to follow.

## Which path is the straight one?

There are several paths available to us—for example, the path of other religions, such as Christianity, Judaism, or Hinduism. There are paths to the devil, black magic, false prophets, or false religious leaders. There are dark paths that do not follow any religion at all. How do we find out which path is the Straight Path?

The answer is found in the Qur'ān. If we are living good lives, according to Allāh and His Rasul, then we are following the straight path. We will reach a good place. If we are living bad lives, then we are following the wrong path and we will reach a bad place. Everything we do in this lifetime will determine whether we reach a good place. The straight path is always the right path. The Arabic term for the right path is **rushd**. Allāh has made the right path clear for us. He says:

$$\text{قَد تَّبَيَّنَ ٱلرُّشْدُ مِنَ ٱلْغَيِّ}$$

*...the Right Path has indeed been made distinct from the wrong...* (2:256)

*And surely Allāh is my Rabb and your Rabb, so worship Him. This is the Right Path.* (19:36; 43:64)

Allāh told us to follow the right path. He has shown us which path is the right one. In the past, Allāh sent many nabis and rasūls to show people the right path. Allāh sent Nabi Muhammad to show all of mankind the right path. Nabi Muhammad, himself, followed the path taught by Allāh. Nabi Muhammad set examples to show us the right path. His examples are called the **Sunnah**.

## The right or wrong way

In everything we do in our lives, there is a right way and a wrong way. If we do things the right way, this means we are on the right path. Praying to Allāh is the right way to practice religion; praying to an idol is the wrong way. Earning money by doing honest work is the right way; making money by cheating and stealing is the wrong way. Being nice to others is the right way; being mean to others is the wrong way. Laughing at others, bullying someone at school, or calling someone insulting names is the wrong way. Treating people with respect and dignity is the right way. When we speak the truth, it is the easiest way. If we lie, we have to work hard and possibly tell more lies to make others believe us. The wrong path is not easy at all.

## The balanced path

The right path is also a **balanced path**. A balanced path does not lead us to extreme actions. In Islam, we should maintain balance in everything we do. An excess of anything is bad.

Eating good food in healthy amounts is the balanced way. Eating too much or too little is not a balanced way. We can become unhealthy if we do not eat the right kind of food. If we eat harām food, which is the wrong path, we are more likely to become unhealthy. Drinking alcohol and smoking is not good for our health or our faith.

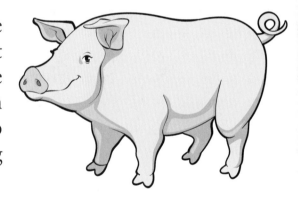

1. Fill in the blanks with two different words.

   A. The right path is a _____ path.

   B. The right path is a _____ path.

2. What is the meaning of the word rushd? _____

Our parents, teachers, imams, and all believers know which path is the right and balanced path. When our parents tell us not to do something or not to go somewhere, they are telling us the right path. If we always follow the teachings of Rasūlullāh, then we cannot follow the wrong path. If we follow the Qur'ān, Allāh will inspire us to follow the right path.

## Prayer to guide us

The beginning of this chapter mentions ayah 6 from sūrah Fātihah. Every day, we recite sūrah Fātihah during our salāt. When we recite ayah 6, we are actually praying to Allāh to guide us on the straight path. This path is a balanced path, and it carries blessings and rewards from Allāh. As mentioned previously, all past nabis and rasūls followed the straight path. All the true believers followed the right path. They all tested this path. From their experiences, we know this path will lead us to the best things in this life and in the **Hereafter**. Allāh always rewards those who walk on the right path.

### Critical thinking

Shaitān wants to derail us from the right path. He is constantly tempting us to forget our duties. When it is time for salāt, he puts lots of excuses in your mind to make you forget or delay salāt. But with a little effort, you can reject Shaitān's ideas. The next time the call for salāt is made, do not delay. All you need to do is take small steps to remain on the right path.

The straight path can lead us to the best ending, which is life in Heaven.

1. Every day, we recite a sūrah asking Allāh﷾ to show us the right and straight path. What is the name of the sūrah?

_____

2. Where will the right path lead us?

_____

3. How do we know which path is the right one?

_____

_____

4. Circle **T** if the sentence is true. Circle **F** if the sentence is false.

The right path has been made clearly visible from the wrong path.　**T**　**F**

Only a few prophets followed the right path.　**T**　**F**

The right path is a balanced and straight path.　**T**　**F**

The right path is an imaginary path, therefore, we cannot follow it.　**T**　**F**

If we want to go to Heaven, we should avoid the right path.　**T**　**F**

5. Mark the box with a ☑ if the sentence is true. Mark the box with an ☒ if the sentence is false.

The right and straight path is the easiest path.　☐

If a certain food is good, we should eat a lot of it.　☐

We should follow the right path in all of our activities.　☐

The Qur'ān and Sunnah are not clear about the right path.　☐

6. The Sunnah of Nabi Muhammad ﷺ tells us to walk on a certain path. Which path does it tell us to walk?

_____

7. Who tested the right path as the best path for us to follow?

    A. The messengers and believers.

    B. The messengers and jinn.

    C. Only the imams.

    D. Only the angels.

8. In order to learn how to walk on the right path we should read two books. What are these two books?

    A. _____

    B. _____

# Unit 3: Nabi Muhammad ﷺ

The three lessons in this unit are devoted to taking a closer look at Nabi Muhammad ﷺ. Our Nabi ﷺ lived his life according to the Qur'ān. He demonstrated practically everything Allāh ﷻ taught us to do, so his actions became examples for mankind to follow. Every action that Nabi Muhammad ﷺ took could be a detailed lesson, however, his kindness is discussed in Lesson 13. Everyone loves to be treated with kindness. It is a language that a deaf person can hear, a blind person can see and animals can understand. Lesson 14 adopts a story format to invite students aboard a time machine. The time machine transports students back to Nabi Muhammad's ﷺ time to witness his exemplary conduct. Lesson 15 discusses our relationship with Nabi Muhammad ﷺ—explaining the status of our Nabi ﷺ, and how we respect and respond to him.

**Lesson 13: Kindness of Rasūlullāh ﷺ**

**Lesson 14: How Rasūlullāh ﷺ Treated Others**

**Lesson 15: Our Relationship With Rasūlullāh ﷺ**

# Unit 3: Nabi Muhammad ﷺ

## Kindness of Rasūlullāh ﷺ

Allāh ﷻ directs us to adopt the behavior of our Nabi Muhammad ﷺ as an example. The kindness of Rasūlullāh ﷺ is one of the most distinguishing characteristics of his conduct. Muslims and non-Muslims respected our Nabi ﷺ because of his kindness. Even his strongest enemies were impressed by his kindness. The lesson describes some of the ways Rasūlullāh ﷺ displayed kindness to others.

## How Rasūlullāh ﷺ Treated Others

In this lesson, students will learn about how Nabi Muhammad ﷺ treated people. Whether they were acquaintances, companions, strangers, or enemies, everyone was touched by his compassionate, just, and honorable treatment of others. Using a story format, this chapter offers a view of the daily life of Nabi Muhammad ﷺ.

## Our Relationship With Rasūlullāh ﷺ

It is important to understand our relationship with Nabi Muhammad ﷺ so that we do not reject him or make him equal to God. In the past, people either rejected their nabis or made them equal to God. Our relationship with Rasūlullāh ﷺ is not like the one that exists between a master and his slave. Our relationship with Rasūlullāh ﷺ is like a student-teacher relationship. This lesson takes a deeper look at this relationship.

# Kindness of Rasūlullāh ﷺ

**Objective of the Lesson:**

Allāh ﷻ directs us to adopt the behavior of our Nabi Muhammad ﷺ as an example. The kindness of Rasūlullāh ﷺ is one of the most distinguishing characteristics of his conduct. Muslims and non-Muslims respected our Nabi ﷺ because of his kindness. Even his strongest enemies were impressed by his kindness. The lesson describes some of the ways Rasūlullāh ﷺ displayed kindness to others.

Kindness is the quality of being friendly, understanding, gentle, warm, and caring for others. It is a quality we find in people all over the world. Kindness is like a universal language that everybody can understand. Even animals understand kindness, and they show kindness toward other animals. Wherever there are human beings and animals, there is an opportunity to show kindness. We can find many opportunities to show kindness every day. We only have to keep our eyes open to see these opportunities.

Sometimes it seems like finding kindness is difficult. It appears that the world is so unkind. Sometimes people go out of their way to make life difficult for others when simple acts of kindness are much easier. Everyone loves to be treated with kindness. Sometimes we are having a bad day, and we desperately need kindness. Therefore, we should all try to offer kindness to others.

## Kindness of Rasūlullāh ﷺ

We can follow Rasūlullāh's ﷺ examples to fully understand what kindness is and how we can show kindness. Our Nabi ﷺ is the finest example of a perfect man in all matters of life. Whether we are discussing kindness, courage, generosity, honesty, loyalty, patience, truthfulness, wisdom, or any other good quality, we find it in him. Allāh ﷻ advises us to consider Nabi ﷺ an example for all of us.

*Certainly you have had in the Messenger of Allāh an excellent exemplar for him who is confident of Allāh and the Last Day, and who remembers Allāh much. (33:21)*

## Mercy for all creatures

Allāh ﷻ sent our Nabi ﷺ as a mercy for the entire world. Rasūlullāh ﷺ practiced everything taught in the Qur'ān. He lived his life according to the Qur'ān. Allāh ﷻ wants us to learn and practice everything our Nabi ﷺ demonstrated through his actions. One of the finest examples of Rasūlullāh's ﷺ behavior is his kindness to everyone. Through his actions, he showed that kindness is not simply what we do, but how we affect others. He demonstrated that kindness is not only about being gentle or nice to someone. Kindness is about how our actions benefit someone in a positive way.

## Kindness in speech

Rasūlullāh ﷺ was always kind in his speech. People never heard him speak a harsh word. Even if something annoyed him, he never spoke harsh words at others. A hadīth reports that a companion once asked Rasūlullāh ﷺ to curse some non-believers. He politely replied, "I have not been sent to curse people, but as a mercy to all mankind."

## Kindess to neighbors

Rasūlullāh ﷺ urged his companions and all believers to look after their neighbors and be ready to help them whenever necessary. There are many examples of Rasūlullāhﷺ treating his neighbors with kindness and compassion, even when they were not nice to him.

One hadīth reports that a woman who lived near Rasūlullāhﷺ regularly threw garbage into his yard to annoy him. He cleaned it. One day, Rasūlullāhﷺ walked out of his home and there was no garbage in his yard. After inquiring, he learned the woman was sick and bedridden. Rasūlullāhﷺ visited her and offered any help she might need. This act of kindness made the woman feel very humble.

Rasūlullāhﷺ said, "He who spends the night satisfied, while knowing that his next-door neighbor is hungry, does not truly believe in me."

## Kindness to weak people

A hadīth reports that a man was so terrified and nervous in Rasūlullāh'sﷺ presence that he began to tremble. Seeing the man's condition, Rasūlullāhﷺ smiled and said, "Take it easy on yourself. For indeed, I am the son of a woman who would eat dried meat." He meant that he was a humble person. At that time, rich people ate only fresh meat, while poor people ate dried meat.

Many people in Arabia owned slaves. When asked how to treat slaves, Rasūlullāhﷺ advised them, "Your servants are your brothers. Allāhﷻ has placed them under your care. So, whoever has a slave under him, let him feed the slave out of what he eats himself, and let him clothe him out of what he clothes himself. And, do not compel them to work which will overpower them. But if they need to finish the work, then assist them with it."

To what type of people Nabi Muhammadﷺ is an example?

_____

What did Rasūlullāhﷺ instruct us to do about a hungry neighbor?

_____

## Kind to strangers

Rasūlullāh was kind to everybody. Even strangers experienced his kindness. It is reported that Rasūlullāh once was sitting in the masjid with some of his companions. A **Bedouin** person entered the masjid and began urinating inside the masjid. The companions were very angry and wanted to stop the man. But Rasūlullāh said, "Do not interrupt him." He allowed the man to finish urinating. Then Rasūlullāh called the man over and told him, "The masjid is not the place where one can throw dirt or urinate. The masjid is the place to recite the Qur'ān, glorify God, and pray." Then Rasūlullāh called for a bucket of water and he poured it over the urine.

## Kind to all living things

Many hadīth describe the kindness of Rasūlullāh toward animals. One hadīth reports that Rasūlullāh said, "God prescribed kindness toward everything, so when you slaughter any animal, slaughter it well. When you sacrifice, make your sacrifice good. And let everyone sharpen his weapon and make it easy for the sacrificial animal."

Another hadīth reports that Rasūlullāh once saw a thin, starving camel. He said to the owner of the camel, "Fear Allāh, these are speechless animals. Do not let them stay hungry."

## Kindness to children

There are many examples of Rasūlullāh's kindness toward children. When he lead salāt, sometimes he recited long sūrahs. But if he heard a baby crying, he would shorten the salāt by reciting a few verses from a sūrah. He wanted to make it easier for the mother who was attending the salāt. He was not only kind to the mother, but also to the baby.

Rasūlullāh's eldest daughter was Zainab. Rasūlullāh played with Zainab's young daughter and carried her on his shoulder while he prayed. One time Muslims were doing salāt in the group when the baby cried. Rasūlullāh picked her up and continued to lead the prayer. When he was in the sujud position, he placed her on the ground. When he stood up for new rak'at of salāt, he picked her up again.

On another occasion, Rasūlullāh was leading salāt. When he was in the sujud position, his young grandson, al-Hasan, climbed on his back. Rasūlullāh lengthened the sujud until al-Hasan climbed down from his back. After Rasūlullāh completed the salāt, he apologized to the group saying, "Verily this son of mine [pointing at al-Hasan] climbed on my back, and I disliked the idea of raising my head until he got down."

## Kind to his enemies

There are many examples of Rasūlullāh's kindness to his enemies. After the Battle of Badr, Muslims captured about 70 prisoners of war. They were brought to Madīnah. Among the prisoners was Rasūlullāh's uncle, al-Abbas. He was not wearing a shirt. Rasūlullāh wanted to find a shirt for him. Rasūlullāh's shirt would not fit his uncle, but his companion's shirt would fit his uncle. Rasūlullāh asked his companion to give the shirt to his uncle. Then Rasūlullāh gave his own shirt to the companion.

The prisoners were treated and fed well. None of them were tortured. Rasūlullāh told his companions, "They are your brothers. Offer them what you eat and drink." The prisoners were allowed to pay money as ransom and return to Makkah. Those who did not have money to

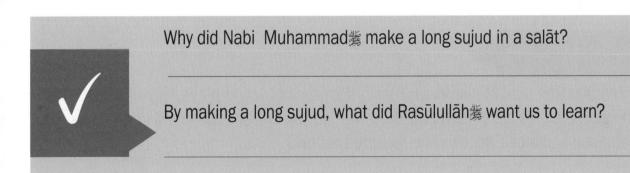

Why did Nabi Muhammad make a long sujud in a salāt?

_____

By making a long sujud, what did Rasūlullāh want us to learn?

_____

pay ransom were released by Rasūlullāhﷺ. Those who knew how to read and write were told to teach reading and writing to children in Madīnah. Then they were allowed to return to Makkah.

There are so many examples of Rasūlullāh'sﷺ kindness. We should not simply listen to these examples and forget them. We should learn from these examples and always try our best to be kind to everyone.

It is reported that that Nabi Muhammadﷺ said: "If any one of you improve (follows strictly) his Islamic religion then his good deeds will be rewarded ten times to seven hundred times for each good deed and a bad deed will be recorded as it is."

1. Mark the box with a ☑ if the sentence is true. Mark the box with an ☒ if the sentence is false.

Rasūlullāhﷺ was kind to everybody—men, women, and children. ☐

Kindness is something that even animals can understand. ☐

If Rasūlullāhﷺ heard a baby crying, he lengthened salāt. ☐

During Rasūlullāh'sﷺ time, women participated in group salāt. ☐

Sometimes Rasūlullāhﷺ cursed those who did something wrong. ☐

Allāhﷻ sent Rasūlullāhﷺ as an example for all mankind. ☐

2. When a boy climbed on Rasūlullāh'sﷺ back during salāt, how did the Nabiﷺ react?

    A. He was upset.

    B. He left the salāt.

    C. He did not get up until the boy climbed down from his back.

    D. He told the parents to never let it happen again.

3. When a woman threw garbage in Rasūlullāh'sﷺ yard, what did he do?

    A. He threw it back in her yard.

    B. He told her not to do it again.

    C. He complained to a local leader.

    D. He cleaned it up.

4. To which of the following groups was Rasūlullāhﷺ kind?

    A. To Animals.

    B. To children

    C. To enemies.

    D. To all of the above.

5. What did Rasūlullāhﷺ say about someone who spends the night satisfied, while knowing that his next-door neighbor is hungry?

_____

6. Circle **T** if the sentence is true. Circle **F** if the sentence is false.

| | | |
|---|---|---|
| Rasūlullāhﷺ made the prisoners of war stay hungry. | **T** | **F** |
| Nabiﷺ said the weapons used to sacrifice animals should be sharp. | **T** | **F** |
| When a Bedouin urinated in the masjid, Nabiﷺ punished him. | **T** | **F** |
| Our Nabiﷺ is the finest example of a perfect man in all matters. | **T** | **F** |
| Rasūlullāhﷺ told people to treat their slaves with kindness. | **T** | **F** |

7. When Rasūlullāhﷺ saw a thin, starving camel, what did he tell the owner of the camel?

_____

# How Rasūlullāh ﷺ Treated Others

**Objective of the Lesson:**

In this lesson, students will learn about how Nabi Muhammad ﷺ treated people. Whether they were acquaintances, companions, strangers, or enemies, everyone was touched by his compassionate, just, and honorable treatment of others. Using a story format, this chapter offers a view of the daily life of Nabi Muhammad ﷺ.

Buckle up, boys and girls! We are riding in a Time Machine that will take us across the ocean and over the mountains.

This machine will take us back to Madīnah during Rasūlullāh's ﷺ lifetime. Let us imagine that our Time Machine can become invisible. Now we, the invisible kids, are following Rasūlullāh ﷺ!

*Certainly you have in the Messenger of Allāh an excellent example to follow... (Surah Al-Ahzab 33:21)*

## A role model

Now that we have arrived in Madīnah, we can see many people trying to follow Rasūlullāh's ﷺ example. They are trying to live like Rasūlullāh ﷺ because he is a role model for everyone.[33:21] So, who is a role model? A role model is a very good person, and we should try to live the same way he or she lives. Just like the people we see around Rasūlullāh, we should also try to have the same qualities.[3:32, 132]

## Would he love us?

Now that we are following him around, we see that he is smiling and playing with kids our age. He is very kind to orphans.[2:220, 93:9, 107:2] An orphan is a child who has lost both parents. So, our Nabi was an orphan, too.[93:6] When Rasūlullāh was a young boy, his mother died. He never saw his father, because his father had passed away before he was born. We can also see that he is very kind to poor people.[89:18] We also see that he advises people to treat the slaves as their brothers and feed and clothe them as they feed and clothe themselves.

## Polite

Luckily our Time Machine moves fast. It is becoming difficult to keep up with Rasūlullāh. He is very busy! We see that he is telling people to lead a good life. He is praying. He is inviting everyone to become a Muslim.[3:63] Some people are following his good advice. Some people are not listening to him. Rasūlullāh is worried about them. Watch out, some of them are mean! They are saying terrible things. Is Rasūlullāh mad at these people? No, he is polite. He pardons them and walks away.[5:13] He was not afraid. By walking away, he gave them a chance to think it over.

## Proud? Not him!

At a gathering with Rasūlullāh, we see that Muslims highly respect him. This respect does not make him a proud man. He is a simple, friendly person.[25:7-8] He always thinks of others. When Muslims faced great difficulty in Makkah, he sent them to live in Madīnah. When he knew the Muslims were safe, only then Rasūlullāh moved to Madīnah.

## Wow, so many people!

As we watch him from our Time Machine, we see that many people are visiting Rasūlullāh. Some of them are not Muslim. Some people need help to solve their problems. Some people want to learn and talk about religion.[3:159] We see that Rasūlullāh speaks to them in a nice way,[16:125] and they like to listen to him. Some non-Muslims visit him to argue, but he is still polite.[29:46]

## In his home

As we follow him throughout the day, we notice that Rasūlullāh makes time for his family. He is a good father and a good husband. We see his daughter, Fatimah (ra), is enjoying his company. We see that Nabi Muhammad loves and respects his wives and other family members.[66:1-6]

## Shhh! It's night-time

After a long day of traveling, we feel tired in the Time Machine. The town of Madīnah becomes dark. The candles and the lamps are blown out. Through our sleepy eyes, we see that Rasūlullāh is praying again. While the town sleeps, he keeps on praying. While our eyes are closing, he and some of his followers are still praying to Allāh.[73:20]

## Last few hours

When we wake up, we see that the Time Machine has taken us back another 30 years. We see a group of travelers arriving at a market. This place does not look like Madīnah! Oh, this is Syria! The travelers gather around Rasūlullāh, who is a young businessman. Here, nobody calls him Rasul or Nabi. We realize that he has not become a nabi yet. But people do call him Al-Amin, the trustworthy.[81:21] Sellers and buyers are flocking around him. They know he never cheats them.

## We are back home!

The fuel in our Time Machine is running out. Now we are back in our own time and our own homes. We clearly saw that Rasūlullāh had many good qualities. We decide to learn about the good qualities that he had and to treat others the way he treated them.[7:158]

*Say: "O you mankind! Surely I am the Rasul of Allāh to you all, to Whom belongs the control of the heavens and the earth. There is no deity but He; He gives life and He gives death. So, believe in Allāh and in His Rasul, the Nabi, the Ummi who believes in Allāh and His Words; and you follow him so that you may be guided." (Surah al-A'raf 7:158)*

## from Hadīth

Rasūlullāh said: "If you love the poor and bring them near you, then Allāh will bring you near Him on the Day of Judgment."

1.  Mark the box with a ☑ if the sentence is true. Mark the box with an ☒ if the sentence is false.

Rasūlullāhﷺ did not like the orphans. ☐

Rasūlullāhﷺ was a good role model, so everyone should follow his example. ☐

When Rasūlullāhﷺ was six years old, his father died. ☐

Rasūlullāhﷺ was polite to bad people. ☐

Rasūlullāhﷺ prayed for hours during the night. ☐

2. Write four things you learned about how our Rasūlﷺ behaved with other people.

1. _____

2. _____

3. _____

4. _____

3. When people visited Rasūlullāhﷺ to talk, how did he speak to them?

_____

4. How did Rasūlullāh☼ treat his wives and other family members?

_____

5. How did Rasūlullāh☼ treat orphans?

   A. He loved them very much.
   B. He did not care for them.
   C. He was rude to them.
   D. He was strict with them.

6. How old was Rasūlullāh☼ when his father passed away?

   A. He was six years old.
   B. He was ten years old.
   C. He was a young man.
   D. His father passed away before Muhammad☼ was born.

7. When Rasūlullāh☼ was a young man, what title did people give him for his truthfulness?

   A. Rasūlullāh.
   B. Al-Amin.
   C. Al-Kalam.
   D. Al- Madīnah.

# Our Relationship With Rasūlullāh ﷺ

**Objective of the Lesson:**

It is important to understand our relationship with Nabi Muhammad ﷺ so that we do not reject him or make him equal to God. In the past, people either rejected their nabis or made them equal to God. Our relationship with Rasūlullāh ﷺ is not like the one that exists between a master and his slave. Our relationship with Rasūlullāh ﷺ is like a student-teacher relationship. This lesson takes a deeper look at this relationship.

Allāh ﷻ is our creator. We are His servants. Our relationship with Allāh ﷻ is that of between a Master and His servant. A servant works under the master and does everything the master wants. A servant does everything possible to please the master. In return for the service, the master feeds and clothes the servant and provides him or her shelter. If a servant disobeys his or her master, the master punishes the servant.

We are Allāh's ﷻ servants. So we obey our Master. We pray to Him and we submit to Him. We worship Him. If He rewards us, we are happy. If He punishes us, we have to suffer. We cannot question Him. If He feeds us, we are content. If He does not provide for us, we will be hungry. Our good and bad, living and dying—everything is in His hands.

## Our relationship with Rasūlullāh ﷺ

We also have a relationship with our Nabi Muhammad ﷺ. This relationship is not like a master and his servant. Rasūlullāh ﷺ does not feed, clothe, or protect us. We do not pray to Rasūlullāh ﷺ. Our relationship with him is not like a father's with his children. Our relationship with Rasūlullāh ﷺ is more like a student-teacher relationship. Let us take a deeper look at this relationship.

## Rasūlullāh ﷺ is our rasūl

We should understand that Muhammad ﷺ was a human being, a mortal—that is, someone who will eventually die. The Qur'ān says:

$$ قُلْ إِنَّمَآ أَنَا۠ بَشَرٌ مِّثْلُكُمْ $$

*Say, "I am but a human being like you..." (18:110)*
*Muhammad is the rasūl of Allāh. (48:29)*

In many places in the Qur'ān, Rasūlullāh ﷺ was told to declare his status. For example,

*Say: "Glory be to my Rabb! Am I anything but a human being, a rasūl." (17:93)*

Even those among the Makkan Quraish who did not believe in Rasūlullāh ﷺ, admitted that he was simply a human being.

*"Is not this [person] anything but a human being like you?" (21:3)*

Two things are important to understand. First, people do not select rasūls. A person cannot decide to become a rasūl. Only Allāh ﷻ appoints a rasūl. This means Muhammad ﷺ did not become a rasūl on his own. Allāh ﷻ chose him. Second, Muhammad ﷺ is the final rasūl. No new nabis or rasūls will be sent. The practice of Allāh ﷻ sending rasūls ended with Muhammad ﷺ.

## Rasūlullāh ﷺ is not our God

One simple meaning of the word rasūl is "messenger." The word Rasūlullāh means "Rasūl of Allāh." A messenger of God is one who shares God's words with people. Muhammad ﷺ is Rasūlullāh because he received God's words and shared them with people.

When we say Shahadah, we declare two important points: (1) who Allāh ﷻ is, and (2) the role of Muhammad ﷺ.

**1** اَشْهَدُ اَنْ لَّا اِلٰهَ اِلَّا اللّٰهُ     No god but Allāh

**2** وَاَشْهَدُ اَنَّ مُحَمَّدً اعَبْدُهُ وَرَسُوْلُهُ     Muhammad is His servant and messenger.

We do not pray to Muhammad ﷺ. He is not a god. Allāh ﷻ declares that Muhammad ﷺ is His servant and a messenger. We should understand that Muhammad ﷺ is not the giver or provider. Only Allāh ﷻ is the giver and provider.

Muhammad ﷺ is God's servant and messenger, therefore, we do not disrespect him in any manner. We show great respect for him, but we do not worship him. Allāh ﷻ teaches us to obey Muhammad ﷺ. Allāh ﷻ showers blessings upon our Nabi and so does the angels. Allāh ﷻ also teaches us to respect our Nabi ﷺ and to pray to Allāh ﷻ to shower him with blessings.

إِنَّ ٱللَّهَ وَمَلَٰٓئِكَتَهُۥ يُصَلُّونَ عَلَى ٱلنَّبِىِّ يَٰٓأَيُّهَا ٱلَّذِينَ ءَامَنُوا۟ صَلُّوا۟ عَلَيْهِ وَسَلِّمُوا۟ تَسْلِيمًا ٥٦

*Surely Allāh and His angels shower blessings upon the Nabi. O you who believe! you seek blessings upon him [Muhammad], and salute with a salutation. (33:56)*

Nabi Muhammadﷺ is our guide and teacher, but what he is not?

_____

What is one thing that Rasūlullāhﷺ cannot give us?

_____

## Rasūlullāhﷺ is our teacher

Rasūlullāhﷺ is our teacher. He showed us everything that a good Muslim should do. His life was an example of everything taught in the Qur'ān. Allāhﷺ says that in our Nabiﷺ is a good example for us to follow.

> *Certainly you have had in the Rasūl of Allāh an excellent example for him who is confident of Allāh and the Future day, and who remembers Allāh much. (33:21)*

Rasūlullāhﷺ taught us how to lead a good life as it is taught in the Qur'ān. The list of things he taught us is long, but some of them are mentioned below. Rasūlullāhﷺ taught us:

1. How to pray.
2. How to be kind, considerate, merciful, forgiving, and just.
3. How to behave with parents, women, children, orphans, the poor, the elderly, the sick, and neighbors.
4. How to give zakāt and how much to give.
5. How to speak and listen to people.
6. How to avoid arrogance and have an open mind about everything.
7. How to stand up against oppression and injustice.
8. How to negotiate a deal with others.
9. How to manage and balance everything in life.
10. How to keep trust [amanat] of others and respect their privacy.

11. How to treat our enemies.

12. In case of war, what to do and what not to do.

13. How to be a good citizen.

14. The right way to earn a living and make transactions.

Long before Muhammadﷺ was a rasūl, he was always truthful. One time he went to Syria to conduct business for Khadījah (ra). He conducted the business with utmost sincerity—he did not cheat customers or his employer; he did not short-change anyone; he did not sell a poor product at a high price. He was kind and polite with customers.

## How to behave with Rasūlullāhﷺ

When the Qur'ān was being revealed, the people of Makkah and Madīnah learned how they should behave toward Rasūlullāhﷺ. Although Rasūlullāhﷺ is no longer with us, we can still learn from these teachings.

When Rasūlullāhﷺ was alive, many people visited him daily to listen to him, to ask questions, or to seek his advice. The Qur'ān advised people on how they should approach Rasūlullāhﷺ.

Sometimes people forgot the Rasūlullāhﷺ was a husband and father, who needed time with his family. Sometimes people knocked on Rasūlullāh'sﷺ back door to speak to him. The Qur'ān advises people not to do this, and to show patience until he stepped out of his home.[48:4] Sometimes, people presented their opinion to Rasūlullāhﷺ without being asked. They were told not to advance their opinion unless they were asked, because he might be receiving divine revelation at that time.[48:1] They were also told not to speak louder than Rasūlullāhﷺ. They were advised not to speak loudly to him, and to speak in a gentle manner.

The Qur'ān also teaches us that Rasūlullāh'sﷺ wives are like our mothers. Just as we show respect for our own mothers, we should show similar respect for his wives. There are several reasons why the Qur'ān never compared Rasūlullāhﷺ as our "father." One reason is to prevent the so-called "sons" to take undue advantage of religion. Another reason is to prevent the so-called "sons" from pretending to be religious leaders.

We should remember that Rasūlullāhﷺ is our teacher. If we want to do well in our life we must listen to the way our "teacher" told us to lead a life. Our "teacher" showed us the path—the path that is blessed. He himself walked on the path. Many other good people walked on the same path. We can pray to Allāhﷻ to guide us in the path that our Nabi Muhammadﷺ followed.

$$ اهْدِنَا الصِّرَاطَ الْمُسْتَقِيمَ ۝ صِرَاطَ الَّذِينَ أَنْعَمْتَ عَلَيْهِمْ غَيْرِ الْمَغْضُوبِ عَلَيْهِمْ وَلَا الضَّالِّينَ ۝ $$

*Guide us on the Right Path,—the path of those upon whom You have bestowed favors; not of those upon whom wrath is brought down, nor of those gone-astray. (1:6–7)*

1. Which of the following statements about Rasūlullāhﷺ is correct?

    A.  Rasūlullāhﷺ is our master and we are his servants.

    B.  Khadijah (ra) made Muhammadﷺ a rasūl.

    C.  The Makkan Quraish believed Rasūlullāhﷺ was an angel.

    D.  Rasūlullāhﷺ was a human being just like us.

2.  During Rasūlullāh'sﷺ lifetime, how did some people approach his house?

    A.  They ringed the bell.

    B.  They knocked on his back door.

    C.  They blew a horn to draw his attention.

    D.  They simply entered his bedroom.

3. When we declare Shahadah, what do we declare about Muhammadﷺ?

_____

4.  Mark the box with a ☑ if the sentence is true. Mark the box with an ☒ if the sentence is false.

People were told not to speak louder than Rasūlullāhﷺ. ☐

Angels did not shower blessings on Rasūlullāhﷺ. ☐

More nabis will be sent after Rasūlullāhﷺ. ☐

Rasūlullāhﷺ is not the giver or provider; Allāhﷺ is the giver and provider. ☐

5. Verse 33:56 of the Qur'ān is quoted in the lesson. In this verse, what does Allāh﷾ wants us to do for Rasūlullāhﷺ?

_____

6. Which of the following statements is incorrect?

    A. We do not disrespect Rasūlullāhﷺ in any manner.

    B. We can pray directly to Rasūlullāhﷺ to protect us.

    C. When Rasūlullāhﷺ conducted business, he was honest.

    D. Rasūlullāhﷺ is Allāh's﷾ servant and a rasūl.

# Unit 4: Messengers of Allah

In this unit, students will learn about the lives and activities of some of the past messengers. These stories provide an engaging learning experience for young readers. The first chapter focuses on the lives of Ismāʿīl (A) and Ishāq (A)—the two illustrious sons of nabi Ibrāhīm (A). The next lesson offers an overview of is about nabi Shuʿaib (A) who attempted to guide a community that was practicing unethical business methods. Shuʿaib (A) tried his best to make the people believe in Allāh and adopt ethical business practices. The third chapter focuses on Dāwūd (A) and his efforts to guide the Children of Israel who were struggling to defeat their enemies. The final lesson in this unit tells the story of ʿIsā (A)—a messenger who also tried to guide the Children of Israel. Students will learn about his life and mission.

**Lesson 16: Ismāʿīl (A) and Ishāq (A):** *Nabi of Allāh*

**Lesson 17: Shuʿaib (A):** *Nabi of Allāh*

**Lesson 18: Dāwūd (A):** *Nabi of Allāh*

**Lesson 19: ʿIsā (A):** *Nabi of Allāh*

# Unit 4: Messengers of Allāhﷻ

## Ismā'īl (A) and Ishāq (A): *Nabi of Allāh*ﷻ

In this lesson, students will learn about Ibrāhīm's (A) two illustrious sons— Isma'il (A) and Ishaq (A). Both became nabi when they were adults. Students will learn about these two nabi—including their birth and their contribution to future generations.

## Shu'aib (A): *Nabi of Allāh*ﷻ

In this chapter, students will learn about a nabi named Shu'aib (A) who lived in northern Arabia. He worked in a trading community that conducted business with travelers. Shu'aib (A) taught people to be fair and honest in their business transactions and not to short-change customers. The lesson provides an overview of his life and teachings, which are still valid today.

## Dāwūd (A): *Nabi of Allāh*ﷻ

The life and mission of nabi Dāwūd (A) are fascinating. He lived during a time when the Children of Israel had leadership problems and external threats from enemies. Students will learn how these problems were solved, and how Dāwūd became a king. They will also read a short summary of the major achievements of this nabi.

## 'Isā (A): *Nabi of Allāh*ﷻ

The final nabi from the lineage of Ishāq (A) was 'Isā (A). 'Isā (A) was a nabi for the Children of Israel, but they rejected him. 'Isa (A) confirmed the teachings of the Tawrāt and also delivered the Injil. This lesson provides a short summary of the life and mission of nabi 'Isā (A).

# Ismāʿīl (A) and Ishāq (A): *Nabi of Allāh*

### Objective of the Lesson:

In this lesson, students will learn about Ibrāhīm's (A) two illustrious sons— Ismaʿil (A) and Ishaq (A). Both became nabi when they were adults. Students will learn about these two nabi—including their birth and their contribution to future generations.

Thousands of years ago, nabi Ibrāhīm (A) was born in Iraq. He spent his early youth in Iraq. His father was an idol worshipper. Ibrāhīm (A) tried to convince his father to give up idol-worshipping, but the father continued to worship idols. Ibrāhīm's (A) father told him to stop disrespecting the idols. He even told Ibrāhīm (A) that if he did not stop disrespecting the idols, then he would throw Ibrāhīm (A) out of his home. Ibrāhīm (A) left home and traveled to different places. He left Iraq and traveled thousands of miles to settle in Egypt. Years passed and he grew older, but he still did not have a child. When he was younger, he had prayed to Allāh﷾ to give him a son. He did not lose his patience. He believed that one day, Allāh﷾ would give him a son.

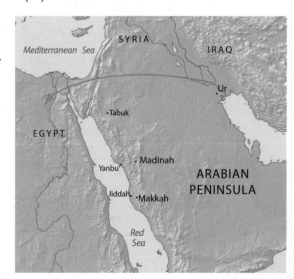

## Birth of Ismā'īl (A)

Ibrāhīm's (A) wife was **Sarah**. She felt sad because they did not have any children. She told Ibrāhīm (A) to marry a woman named **Hajar**. After Ibrāhīm (A) married Hajar, they had a son. His name was **Ismā'īl** (A). Before he was born, both Hajar and Sarah were friends. After Ismā'īl (A) was born, it is reported that Sarah began to feel jealous of Hajar.

Ibrāhīm (A) noticed that his family was experiencing tension. In order to maintain family peace, Ibrāhīm (A) decided Hajar and Ismā'īl (A) should live far away from Egypt. This relocation plan was based on guidance from Allāh.

## Allāh's plan

Allāh had a plan for Ismā'īl (A) and his mother. Inspired by Allāh, Ibrāhīm (A) began traveling with his wife Hajar, and their newborn child, Ismā'īl (A), hundreds of miles through Arabia. Along the way, they crossed some of the fertile lands of Arabia and some of the cooler areas full of date trees and water wells. Ibrāhīm (A) did not consider these places ideal for his family. Finally, they reached a valley near some mountain. This area was full of granite rocks, and no one lived there. But Ibrāhīm (A) believed it was the right place for his family to settle down.

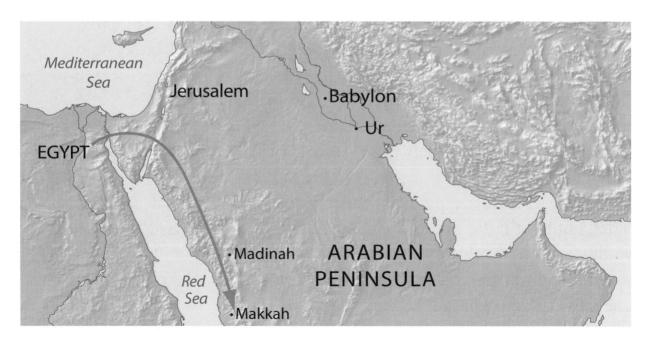

This area is called **Bakkah** in the Qur'ān. Bakkah contained one special feature—the ruins of a stone structure. It was the first structure nabi Ādam (A) built to worship Allāh. Ibrāhīm (A) helped his family settle there. He prayed to Allāh to keep the area safe and to provide its people with fruit.[2:126] He also prayed to save him and his children from worshipping idols.[14:35] Later, Bakkah became known as **Makkah**.

## Birth of Ishāq (A)

Many years after the birth of Ismā'īl (A), Ibrāhīm (A) had another son. When Ibrāhīm (A) was very old, some angels came to see him and his wife Sarah. The angels told them that Allāh was going to give them a son, and a grandson. They said the son would be named **Ishāq** (A), and the grandson would be named **Ya'qub** (A).

Sarah could not believe it and she laughed. She thought she was too old. The angels told them not to wonder about Allāh's decision. Allāh's mercy and blessings were upon them. When Sarah gave birth to a son, they named him Ishāq (A). He grew up to be a great nabi. Ishāq's son, Ya'qub (A) also became a great nabi.

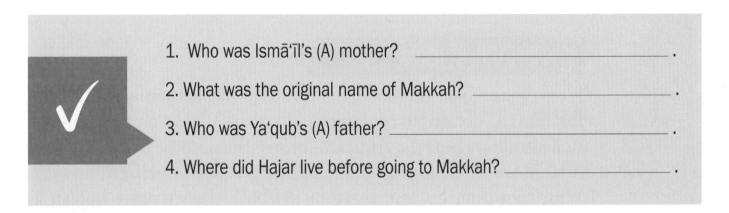

1. Who was Ismā'īl's (A) mother? _____.

2. What was the original name of Makkah? _____.

3. Who was Ya'qub's (A) father? _____.

4. Where did Hajar live before going to Makkah? _____.

## Ismā'īl (A) in Bakkah

After Ibrāhīm (A) helped his family settle in Bakkah, he returned to Egypt. Soon their water supply ran out. Baby Ismā'īl (A) cried for water, but Hajar did not have any to give him. She hoped to locate some travelers who might have water with them. Hajar climbed a small hill, **Safa**, to look into the distance. She did not see any water or any people. She saw another small hill, **Marwah**. She ran between the two hills looking for water. She became tired and very thirsty. She had left her baby son in an open space nearby. When she returned to her son, she was surprised to find a spring of water at the baby's feet. She gave water to Isma'il (A). This spring of water is known as **Zamzam**. The spring did not stop flowing. It became a constant source of water in the area from that time on.

## People began to arrive

A short time later, a group of Arab travelers was passing through the area. They noticed some birds flying in circles over a certain area. They thought the birds had probably found a water source. When they walked to this area, they found Hajar, Ismā'īl (A), and the Zamzam spring. Later they decided to settle here. Hājar allowed them to settle in Bakkah on the condition that the Zamzam would remain her property. Over time, more people settled in the area.

Eventually, an Arab nation originated from the children of the people who lived in this area. When Ismā'īl (A) grew up, he married a woman from these people.

## Ibrahim (A) visits again

From time to time, Ibrāhīm (A) returned to visit his family in Makkah. Ibrāhīm (A) decided to construct a House of Allāh on the ruins of a stone structure near the Zamzam spring. The purpose of the House of Allāh was to help people develop the practice of performing salāt. With help from his son, Ibrāhīm (A) built the structure known as the Ka'bah. During its construction, Ibrāhīm (A) and Ismā'īl (A) prayed to Allāh to accept their efforts. The du'a they prayed was the following:

$$ رَبَّنَا تَقَبَّلْ مِنَّا إِنَّكَ أَنتَ السَّمِيعُ الْعَلِيمُ ۝ $$

*Our Rabb! Accept from us, surely You, You are all-Hearing, all-Knowing. (2:127)*

Their prayers were accepted immediately. Then Allāhﷻ ordered Ibrāhīm (A) to announce the **Hajj**. After the announcement, people began to arrive in Makkah to do Hajj every year.

## A great sacrifice

When Ismā'īl (A) was a young boy, Ibrāhīm (A) told him about a dream. In the dream, he was sacrificing his son for Allāhﷻ. Ibrāhīm (A) knew it was not a nightmare. It was an order from Allāhﷻ. After hearing about the dream, young Ismā'īl was not afraid. He said he was ready to sacrifice his life for Allāhﷻ. Both father and son prepared for the sacrifice. It was a serious test of faith for both of them. Then Allāhﷻ told them that their intention to sacrifice Ismā'īl's (A) life was good enough. Allāhﷻ told them to sacrifice a ram instead. Every year during **Eid al-Adha**, we sacrifice an animal to remember the serious test of faith of Ibrāhīm (A) and Ismā'īl (A).

## People began to arrive

Allāhﷻ selected Ismā'īl (A) and Ishāq (A) to become nabi. The sons of Ishāq (A) and many of their sons also became nabi. Muhammadﷺ was the only nabi born from one of the sons of Ismā'īl (A).

1. What are the names of the two hills Hajar ran between?

   _____     _____.

2. On which Eid do we sacrifice an animal?   _____.

3. Which nabi was born from the sons of Ismā'īl (A)? _____.

1. Who was Ismā'īl's (A) mother?

   _____

2. Where did Ibrāhīm (A) take his family to live?

   _____

3. What did Ibrāhīm (A) and Ismā'īl (A) build together?

   _____

4. Circle **T** if the sentence is true. Circle **F** if the sentence is false.

   Ibrāhīm's (A) first wife gave birth to Ismā'īl (A).          **T**     **F**

   Hajar ran between Jabal an-Nur and Hira in search of water.     **T**     **F**

   Ismā'īl (A) was afraid to lay down his life for the sake of Allāh.     **T**     **F**

5. Draw a line to match the words in Column A to the correct words in Column B.

   | Column A | Column B |
   |----------|----------|
   | Sarah's son | Spring |
   | Zamzam | Stone house |
   | Ka'bah | Eid al-Adha |
   | Safa and Marwah | Ishāq |
   | Sacrifice | Two hills |

6. Who was the nabi born from the sons of Ismā‘īl (A)?

_____

7. Find the following words in the word search puzzle.

> KABAH    ZAMZAM    HAJAR    MAKKAH
> SARAH    ISMAIL    ISHAQ    SAFA

```
S  B  Z  S  A  R  A  H
A  K  A  B  A  H  W  G
F  T  M  A  K  K  A  H
A  M  Z  I  S  H  A  Q
L  H  A  J  A  R  L  R
I  S  M  A  I  L  C  Z
```

# Shuʻaib (A): *A Nabi of Allāh* ﷻ

**Objective of the Lesson:**

In this chapter, students will learn about a nabi named Shuʻaib (A) who lived in northern Arabia. He worked in a trading community that conducted business with travelers. Shuʻaib (A) taught people to be fair and honest in their business transactions and not to short-change customers. The lesson provides an overview of his life and teachings, which are still valid today.

Long ago, a nabi of Allāh ﷻ lived in northern Arabia. His name was Shuʻaib (A). He lived several generations after Ibrāhīm (A). He is considered an Arabian nabi, because he lived and served in Arabia.

## Madyan

Nabi Shuʻaib (A) lived in **Madyan**. This area is in the northern part of Arabia. This place was important because it connected two significant regions—**Syria** to the north and **Yemen** to the south. For thousands of years, traders traveled between these two regions and passed through Madyan (see map on the next page). They stopped in Madyan to rest and collect food and supplies for their travels. As a result of all these trading activities, Madyan became quite prosperous. However, along with this prosperity came some evil.

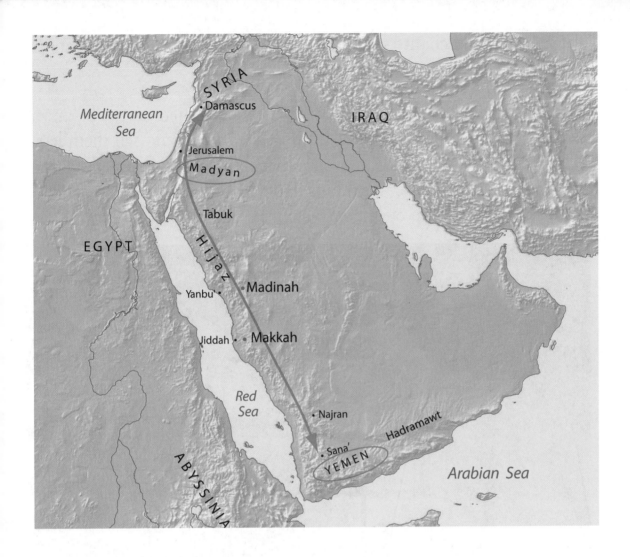

## People of Madyan

After observing the trading activities of the travelers, many people in Madyan started their own businesses. These businesspeople became greedy. They began cheating and robbing the traders.

From the earliest days of human civilization, merchants needed a way to determine the value of goods that could not be counted. For example, grain, corn, and wheat are sold in bulk and cannot be counted. So the merchants invented weighing scales, which were actually balances. They used two plates attached to an overhead beam, which was fixed to a central pole. The measurement was taken by adding the grain or other item on one plate and adding weight-setting stones on the other until the scales balanced. In many parts

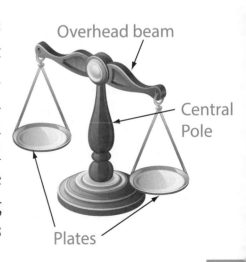

Overhead beam

Central Pole

Plates

of the world, merchants still use such balances today. These balances are available in different sizes and shapes.

The merchants in Madyan began to cheat customers on the balance. When a customer bought goods from them, they would sell them less. When they bought goods from travelers, they took more than the balance indicated. If the merchants had bad or rotten goods, they hid them and sold them to customers when they could.

### Shu'aib (A) advises the merchants

Shu'aib (A) was an honest person living in Madyan. Allāh﷾ chose him to become a nabi and guide the people of Madyan. Shu'aib (A) told his people to worship no one but Allāh﷾.

قَالَ يَـٰقَوْمِ ٱعْبُدُواْ ٱللَّهَ مَا لَكُم مِّنْ إِلَـٰهٍ غَيْرُهُۥ ۖ ٨٥

*He said, "O my people! worship Allāh; you have no deity other than Him..." (7:85)*

As with all previous messengers, Shu'aib's (A) first message cautioned his people to worship only Allāh. Then Shu'aib (A) advised them on proper way to conduct business. He advised them to remember the following:

1. Give the full measure and weight for goods

2. Do not cheat people during transactions.

3. Do not practice corruption or create trouble.

4. Do not ambush travelers.

5. Do not turn away from Allāh's path.

6. Do not make Allāh's path look crooked.

## The leaders objected

The leaders of Madyan objected to Shu'aib's (A) teachings. Sometimes, it appears that community leaders always oppose the truth. When Nūh (A) guided his people, the leaders of his community laughed at him and rejected him. In the same way, the leaders rejected Hūd (A) and Sālih (A). During Nabi Muhammad's time, most of the Quraish leaders opposed him.

In Shu'aib's (A) time, the same thing happened. The leaders rejected the teachings and threatened to throw Shu'aib (A) and other believers out of Madyan. If he wanted to stay, the leaders demanded Shu'aib (A) return to their lifestyle and conduct business their way—by cheating.

The leaders of Madyan were afraid that some people might believe in Shu'aib's (A) teachings. Therefore, they told people that if they followed Shu'aib (A), they would suffer losses. They also spread a false claim that Shu'aib (A) was a liar and a magician. This was not a new strategy. In the past, people had accused other nabis, such as Hūd (A), Salih (A), Mūsā (A), and Muhammad of being liars or magicians.

The leaders said Shu'aib (A) was a weak person—meaning he had no power or status in society. Therefore, the leaders thought people should not follow him. They also said that they would have stoned him to death long ago if it was not for his family.

Shu'aib (A) was shocked to hear this. He replied, "Do you consider my family more honorable than Allāh? In fact, you turn away from Allāh, but you do not know that Allāh is going to punish you for this." Later these people plotted to kill Shu'aib (A).

### Shu'aib (A) prays to Allāh

The leaders of the community turned Shu'aib's (A) life miserable with their threats and taunting comments. The merchants continued to behave corruptly. Then at one point, Shu'aib (A) prayed to Allāh:

*Our Rabb! decide between us and our people with truth, for you are the best of the Deciders." (7:89)*

### Allāh destroys the bad people

Allāh gave the corrupt people enough time to realize their mistakes and become better people. But they had no interest in becoming better people. Then one night, a terrible earthquake destroyed their homes. The destruction was massive and most of the people died.

The earthquake did not affect Shu'aib (A). Allāh saved him and the small number of believers. Allāh always saves the believers.

1. How did the merchants in Madyan conduct business?

_____ .

2. How did the leaders threaten to punish Shu'aib?

_____ .

1. Which two places were important to Madyan, where Shu'aib (A) lived?

    A.  Madīnah and Syria.

    B.  Egypt and Syria.

    C.  Egypt and Palestine.

    D.  Syria and Yemen.

2.  How did the leaders of Madyan treat Shu'aib (A)?

    A.  They treated him well.

    B.  They made him a king.

    C.  They laughed at him and rejected him.

    D.  They sent him to Syria.

3. Mark the box with a ☑ if the sentence is true. Mark the box with an ☒ if the sentence is false.

A massive flood destroyed the people of Madyan. ☐

Shu'aib (A) advised people on the proper way of doing business. ☐

Sometimes people in Madyan ambushed travelers. ☐

Businesspeople in Madyan were mostly honest. ☐

People in Madyan threatened to kill Shu'aib (A). ☐

In Shu'aib's (A) time, Madyan was a very prosperous place. ☐

4. Unscramble the following letters to make meaningful words.

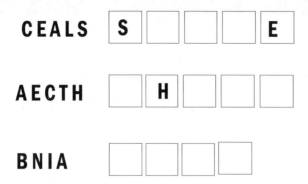

CEALS | S | | | | E

AECTH | | H | | |

BNIA | | | | |

5. The leaders of Madyan said they would have killed Shu'aib (A) but they did not do it because of one thing. What is this one thing?

    A. His brothers.

    B. His wealth.

    C. His business.

    D. His family.

# Dāwūd (A): *A Nabi of Allāh*

**Objective of the Lesson:**

The life and mission of nabi Dāwūd (A) are fascinating. He lived during a time when the Children of Israel had leadership problems and external threats from enemies. Students will learn how these problems were solved, and how Dāwūd became a king. They will also read a short summary of the major achievements of this nabi.

Thousands of years ago, a large group of believers lived in Egypt. They were known as **Bani Isra'il** or "the Children of Israel." Bani Isra'il experienced lots of problems. When they lived in Egypt, Pharaoh tortured them and treated them live like slaves. Then Mūsā (A) rescued them and brought them to Palestine to live.

However, in Palestine, they faced new problems. Around the Palestine region, some ferocious tribes lived. They harassed the Children of Isra'il. They tortured and killed Bani Isra'il and looted their properties. At that time, Bani Isra'il did not have a king. Without a leader, Bani Isra'il could not organize and fight their enemies.

## Talūt becomes king

Bani Isra'il wanted a king who would guide them in how to fight. Their nabi told them to make **Talūt (Saul)** their king. Talūt was a common person, and he did not have wealth. Bani Isra'il were not happy that Talūt was made their king. They thought a king should be someone who had wealth and was well-known. Their nabi told them that wealth is not a reason for someone to become a king. Talūt had other great qualities to make him a good king.

Allāh﷾ gave Talūt knowledge and wisdom. He also gave him courage and strength. All these qualities are necessary for a king to successfully lead a country. Bani Isra'il had no choice but to follow Talūt's leadership. Within a short time, Talūt organized and prepared an army to fight their enemies.

## Dāwūd (A) joins the army

Dāwūd (A) was a young man who joined Talūt's army. One of the enemies was a giant fighter named **Goliath**, or **Jalut**. Everybody was afraid to fight Jalut because he was very strong and powerful. He could kill people with one swing of his sword.

Before actual battle, two or four fighters would fight a **duel**. A duel is a battle between two fighters who use their bare hands or weapons. There are some legends about this battle. One legend says that King Talūt asked his soldiers to challenge Jalut, but nobody came forward. Everyone was afraid. King Talūt offered many rewards to anyone who could defeat Jalut. Still, nobody came forward.

## Dāwūd (A) fights Jalut

Seeing that nobody came forward to fight Jalut, young Dāwūd (A) offered to fight him. The enemies laughed when they saw this young man, who was like a boy. Dāwūd (A) knew that Jalut was strong, but he also knew Allāh﷾ was on the side of the good people. Dāwūd (A) prayed to Allāh﷾ to give him patience and make his feet strong. To

have "strong feet" means to be able to withstand torture and not run away for fear of death.

رَبَّنَا أَفْرِغْ عَلَيْنَا صَبْرًا وَثَبِّتْ أَقْدَامَنَا وَٱنصُرْنَا عَلَى ٱلْقَوْمِ ٱلْكَـٰفِرِينَ ﴿٢٥٠﴾

**Rabbanā afrigh 'alaynā sabrāan wa thabbit aqdāmanā wa ansurnā 'ala-l qawmi-l kāfirīn.**

*Our Rabb! pour down upon us perseverance, and make our feet firm, and help us against the unbelieving people. (Surah Baqarah 2:250).*

There are fascinating details related to the duel between Dāwūd and Jalut. However, the Qur'ān does not mention these details, so we do not know if they are accurate. The Qur'ān simply says Dāwūd (A) killed Jalut. The Qur'ān also says a small army defeated a much larger and stronger army.[2:251] The main reason the smaller army was successful was

1. Who was Talūt?

_____.

2. Who made Talūt a king? _____.

3. In his prayer, what two things did Dāwūd (A) ask for?

_____.

that they had full trust in Allāh. With Allāh's help, every difficulty can be overcome.

## Dāwūd (A) becomes a nabi

Talūt ruled Bani Isra'il for many years. After he died, Dāwūd (A) became the king of Bani Isra'il.

Later, Allāh made Dāwūd (A) a nabi. He sent a divine book named the **Zabur** to Dāwūd (A). Some parts of the Zabur were lost, and some parts are in the Christian Bible.

## Skills of Dāwūd (A)

Dāwūd (A) was a very skillful person. He learned how to smelt iron and used the iron to build shields for his army.[21:80] Using these iron shields in battle made his army became unbeatable. He also understood how to use birds in battle.[34:10] His army included many birds. They carried messages from the battlefield to the king. Also when nabi Dāwūd (A) praised Allāh, the entire mountain echoed his praise.[38:18]

Nabi Dāwūd (A) was known for his fair judgment. One time, some sheep belonging to a shepherd destroyed the crops of a farmer. Dāwūd (A) made a fair judgment to resolve the problems.

Dāwūd (A) had a son named Sulaimān (A). When Dāwūd (A) died, Sulaimān (A) became the king. Allāh made Sulaimān (A) a nabi, too.

1. Memorize the duʻa of Dāwūd (A) and be ready to recite it in front of the class.

2. Why was King Talūt's army afraid of Jalut?

   _____

3. Which book did Allāhﷻ send to prophet Dāwūd (A)?

   _____

4. Draw a line to match the words in Column A to the correct words in Column B.

   | Column A | Column B |
   | --- | --- |
   | Zabur | Shield |
   | Talūt | Giant |
   | Jalut | Prophet |
   | Iron | Book |
   | Sulaimān | King |

5. Dāwūd (A) was skilled in many things. Write three things that he did well.

   1. _____

   2. _____

   3. _____

6. Find the following words in the word search puzzle.

DAWUD  SAUL  SULAIMAN  ZABUR

ALLAH  IRON  TALUT  SHEEP

| B | W | T | A | S | H | E | E | P |
|---|---|---|---|---|---|---|---|---|
| R | R | A | L | L | A | H | B | D |
| A | Y | L | G | I | R | O | N | A |
| N | S | U | C | N | O | X | V | W |
| T | A | T | N | G | H | F | K | U |
| S | U | L | A | I | M | A | N | D |
| E | L | T | Z | A | B | U | R | M |

# 'Isā (A): *A Nabi of Allāh*ﷻ

**Objective of the Lesson:**

The final nabi from the lineage of Ishāq (A) was 'Isā (A). 'Isā (A) was a nabi for the Children of Israel, but they rejected him. 'Isā (A) confirmed the teachings of the Tawrāt and also delivered the Injil. This lesson provides a short summary of the life and mission of nabi 'Isā (A).

Nabi 'Isā (A) was born about 600 years before Nabi Muhammadﷺ. He was as a nabi for the followers of Mūsā (A) and Dāwūd (A). This community was known as the **Bani Isra'il**, or the Children of Israel. In the previous chapter, we learned about Dāwūd (A), who became a king and a nabi for Bani Isra'il. 'Isā (A) was a nabi for the Bani Isra'il, while nabi Muhammadﷺ was a nabi for the entire world. Today, the followers of 'Isā (A) are known as Christians.

## Mother of 'Isa (A)

'Isā's (A) mother was named Maryam. When Maryam was still a child, her mother dedicated her to work in the temple. People who visited the temple to worship Allāhﷻ were very happy to see Maryam's work. The worshippers often brought fruits to the temple. Seeing the large collection of fruits, many people were surprised. People asked Maryam wherefrom she got the fruits. She simply replied, "It is from Allāh." In saying this, she meant that Allāh provides endless food and drinks to whomever He pleases.3:37

Maryam worked in the temple for many years. When she became a young woman, Allāh sent angels to her. They brought some good news. First, they praised Maryam for all her good work. They said, "*Surely Allāh has chosen you and purified you, and chosen you above the women of the nations.*"3:42 This was a great honor. The angels advised her to continue her worship and to pray with those who pray.3:43

Next, the angels told her that she would have a son. Maryam was surprised because she was not married. Then Allāh informed her that He can create as He wishes.3:47

*O Maryam! surely Allāh gives you good news with a Word from Him: His name is the Masih, 'Isā, son of Maryam, who will have dignity in this world and the Hereafter ... (3:45)*

### Birth of 'Isa (A)

After receiving this information about the birth of a son, Maryam moved to the east and gave birth to 'Isā (A). Later she returned to her native place with 'Isā (A). People did not like 'Isā (A) or his mother. The priests accused them of bringing evil and taunted them.[19:27] They refused to speak to 'Isā (A) saying he was a child in the cradle.[19:29]

'Isā (A) told his people that he was a nabi. He received a divine book from Allāh. 'Isā (A) said that making salāt and paying zakāt were made compulsory for him.[19:31] He was very kind to his mother and he was not proud.

## The Injil given to 'Isa (A)

Before 'Isā (A) was born, Allāh had promised Maryam that He would give her son wisdom and knowledge about His books.[3:48] Allāh fulfilled His promise. He sent a book to 'Isā (A) named the **Injil**. He also taught 'Isā (A) the teachings of the **Tawrāt**. The Tawrāt was a divine book sent to Musa (A). 'Isā (A) confirmed the teachings of the Tawrāt. Both the Tawrāt and the Injil contained guidance for the Children of Israel. Nabi 'Isā (A) said that a messenger would be sent who would be the messenger for all of mankind.

## People's reaction

In every age, most people did not like the teachings of their nabis and rasūls. They were rude and mean to them. Many people among the Quraish opposed Nabi Muhammad. People opposed Ibrāhīm (A). The king and his people were mean to Mūsā (A). People were mean to 'Isā (A) too. They refused to listen to him. Even the priests and elders opposed him and taunted him.

## Plan to kill 'Isa (A)

Some of the priests and elders planned to kill 'Isā's (A). We learned previously that the Quraish tried to kill Nabi Muhammad several times, and they fought battles against him. Allāh protected him from being killed. Pharaoh planned to kill nabi Mūsā (A) when he was a newborn baby. People wanted to kill their nabis and rasūls because they did not like their teachings. 'Īsā's (A) people tried to kill him on a cross. People wanted to kill 'Īsā (A) because he opposed their beliefs and advised them to be good people. They did not want to hear his teachings. The Qur'ān says the people could not kill 'Īsā (A), nor could they **crucify** him.[4:157] Allāh saved him.

1. What did the priests say about 'Isa (A) when they saw him?

_____ .

2. What is the name of the book Allāh gave 'Isa (A)?

_____ .

## Not the Son of God

After nabi 'Īsā (A), some people circulated the idea that he had been the Son of God. Many people liked this idea. They began to believe this story. But 'Īsā (A) was not the Son of God. Allāh never had a son or daughter. Allāh said that He cannot have a child since He has no wife.[6:102] Allāh created the nabis and rasūls. They are His servants, not His sons. He is not the father of anyone.

## Teachings of 'Isa (A)

'Īsā (A) told his people to worship only Allāh. As with all other messengers, 'Īsā (A) showed people the Right Path. He was supported by the **Holy Spirit—Ruhul Quddus**—which means Angel Jibril. Angel Jibril brought revelations to Rasūlullāh. Angel Jibril supported all other messengers who received Allāh's message.

Allāh blessed 'Īsā (A) as He had blessed all other messengers. The Qur'ān mentions 'Īsā (A) as the **Masih**, or the blessed one.[3:45]

1. What is the name of the book that Allāh﷽ sent to 'Isa (A)?

_____

2. Angel Jibril (A) supported 'Isa (A). What is another name for Angel Jibril (A)?

_____

3. Nabi 'Isa's (A) people wanted to kill him. The Qur'ān says they failed. What are the two things they could not do to him?

    1. _____

    2. _____

4. What were the two duties that nabi 'Isa (A) said were required for him?

    1. _____

    2. _____

5. The Qur'ān mentions 'Isa (A) by another name. What is the name, and what is the meaning of the name?

Name: _____

Meaning: _____

6. Who was 'Isa's (A) mother?

_____

7. Nabi 'Isa (A) said a messenger would arrive after him. Who was that messenger?

_____

8. Allāh sent 'Isā (A) as a nabi for which community?

   A. The Romans.
   B. The Arabs.
   C. The Children of Israel.
   D. The Children of Pharaoh.

9. 'Isā (A) confirmed which divine book?

   A. The Qur'ān.
   B. The Zabur.
   C. The Tawrāt.
   D. The Hadīth.

10. What did 'Isā (A) say about Muhammadﷺ?

   A. He said Muhammadﷺ would be sent as a Nabi.
   B. He said Muhammadﷺ would be an idol for the Muslims.
   C. He said Muhammadﷺ would follow him.
   D. He said Muhammadﷺ would reject the Injil.

# Unit 5: Learning About Islam

The objective of this unit is to introduce students to some diverse topics about Islam. The concepts discussed in this unit require extensive study. An early understanding of these ideas will allow students to acquire basic information that will help them in future grades. The goal here is to keep it simple and enjoyable, yet informative. Lessons 20 and 21 focus on two of the most important masjids in Islam—the Haram Sharif in Ka'bah and the Masjid in Nabawī. These chapters describe the early construction of the masjid, some historical anecdotes, and later renovations. Lessons 22 and 23 discuss two slaves who accepted Islam and contributed immensely to further the cause of Islam. Knowing just the basics of Islam, Bilāl was committed to his faith despite suffering some of the worst atrocities imaginable. Zayd refused the opportunity to reunite with his father, choosing to remain with his master, Nabi Muhammadﷺ instead. This chapter highlights the historical details of these events.

**Lesson 20: The Ka'bah**

**Lesson 21: Masjid an-Nabawī:** *The Nabi's Masjid*

**Lesson 22: Bilāl ibn Rabāh**

**Lesson 23: Zayd ibn Hārithah**

# Unit 5: Learning About Islam

## The Ka'bah

This lesson provides a short account of the Ka'bah—from the time of its construction until the present time. The chapter describes some of the details about its structure, feature, and role in Muslim life. The Ka'bah unites all Muslims as they pray in the direction of the Ka'bah. Students will learn that Muslims do not worship the Ka'bah, they direct their prayer to Allāh☆.

## Masjid an-Nabawī: *The Nabi's Masjid*

The Masjid an-Nabawī, also known as the Prophet's Mosque, was originally built by Nabi Muhammad☆. It was the residence of Nabi Muhammad☆, a masjid for early Muslims, and later the grave of Nabi Muhammad☆. The history of its early construction is as fascinating, as the history of its future renovations and modifications. Students will learn the basic details about the masjid and its identifying features.

## Bilāl ibn Rabāh

In this lesson, students will learn about Bilāl ibn Rabāh—a black slave and one of the first to accept Islam. He was not forced to accept Islam, but from the little he heard about it, he believed it was a true religion. His uncompromising dedication to Islam is impressive. His life and sacrifices highlight the overall situation in Arabia and the challenges faced by early Muslims.

## Zayd ibn Hārithah

One of the distinguished companions of Rasūlullāh☆ was Zayd Ibn Hārithah. For many years he was known as Rasūlullāh's☆ adopted son. This chapter narrates the early life of Zayd, focusing on how he was sold at a slave market, and how he became part of Rasūlullāh's☆ household. The lesson also describes Rasūlullāh's☆ kindness and compassion toward Zayd.

# The Ka'bah

## Objective of the Lesson:

This lesson provides a short account of the Ka'bah—from the time of its construction until the present time. The chapter describes some of the details about its structure, feature, and role in Muslim life. The Ka'bah unites all Muslims as they pray in the direction of the Ka'bah. Students will learn that Muslims do not worship the Ka'bah, they direct their prayer to Allāhﷻ.

In a previous grade, we learned about the Five-Pillars of Islam. The fifth pillar is Hajj or pilgrimage to Makkah. The most important monument in Makkah is the Ka'bah. It is a simple structure, but it is the most important structure for Muslims all over the world. Muslims pray five times a day. All these prayers are performed toward a **qiblah**, or direction. This qiblah is the Ka'bah. It is important to understand that Muslims do not offer their salāt to the Ka'bah. They face the direction of the Ka'bah and their salāt is offered to Allāhﷻ.

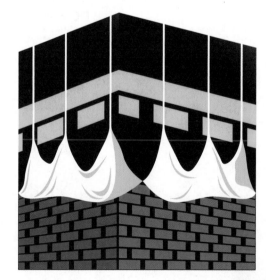

## Early history of the Ka'bah

The Qur'ān states the Ka'bah was re-built by Ibrāhīm (A) and his son Ismā'īl (A). According to Islamic belief, Adam (A) built the original Ka'bah. Over the course of time, the structure broke down except its foundation remained. Due to Allāh's inspiration, Ibrāhīm (A) chose the area near the Ka'bah for his family to live. Also with Allāh's inspiration, Ibrāhīm (A) re-built the Ka'bah with his son Ismā'īl (A).[22:26] It is believed that the original Ka'bah was a four-wall structure without a roof.

Allāh identified the Ka'bah as "my house" and asked that the structure be dedicated for tawāf and salāt. While raising the structure of the Ka'bah, Ibrāhīm (A) prayed to Allāh to accept their efforts.

$$رَبَّنَا تَقَبَّلْ مِنَّا ۖ إِنَّكَ أَنتَ ٱلسَّمِيعُ ٱلْعَلِيمُ ﴿١٢٧﴾$$

*Our Rabb! Accept from us, You indeed, You are the all-Hearing, all-Knowing. (2:127)*

Allāh accepted this prayer and made Hajj an annual event for people in and around Arabia. This event shows us that Allāh always accepts sincere du'a. We should learn this du'a. Whenever we begin new work, large or small, we should use this du'a to pray Allāh.

## Structure of the Ka'bah

The Ka'bah is a large building made of nicely shaped black granite rocks. These rocks came from the hills near Makkah. The Ka'bah is not shaped like a square, but it looks like a square structure. The four corners of the Ka'bah match the four directions of a compass—east, west, north, and south. Each corner has its own name.

Western corner:  Rukn as-Shām, or the Syrian Corner

Eastern corner:  Rukn al-Aswad, or the Black Corner

Southern corner: Rukn al-Yamani, or the Yemeni Corner

Northern corner: Rukn al-Irāqi, or the Iraqi Corner

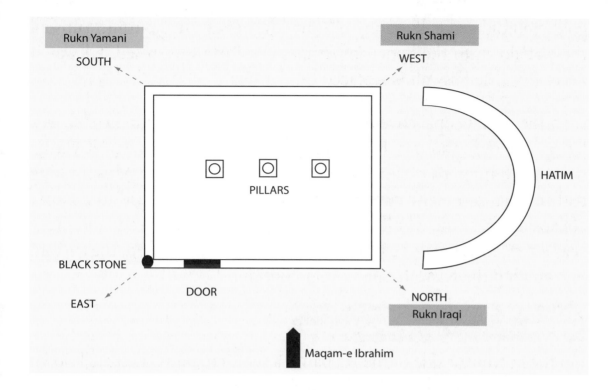

In the eastern corner, there is a black stone. This stone is known as **Hajr al-Aswad**. It is possibly a meteorite. During Hajj or 'Umrah, people perform seven rounds of tawāf around the Ka'bah. Each cycle of tawāf begins from the eastern corner where the Hajr al-Aswad is located.

The inside of the Ka'bah is empty. Three pillars support the roof. People are not permitted to enter the Ka'bah except for special reasons, such as make repairs. The lower interior walls are covered with marble slabs that extend halfway to the roof. The upper half is covered with green cloth embroidered with Qur'ānic verses. The marbles are also engraved with Qur'ānic verses. The floor inside the Ka'bah is made of marble and limestone.

There is a door on the north-eastern wall of the Ka'bah. The doorway is elevated a few feet above the ground to prevent floodwater from entering the Ka'bah.

## Kiswah

The Ka'bah is covered by a black silk curtain known as the **Kiswah**. About two-thirds of the way up on the curtain, there is a band of gold-embroidered calligraphy of Qur'ānic verses. This curtain runs all the way down to the floor. Sometimes the curtain is raised halfway if necessary. The Kiswah is replaced once a year.

In the past, people covered the Ka'bah with various kinds of sheets, lacing one over another. If a sheet became old, they covered it with a new one. Hundreds of years after Nabi Muhammadﷺ, a Muslim king realized that too many coverings on the Ka'bah might lead to the roof collapsing. He ordered all the old coverings to be removed, and every year a new covering to be placed on the Ka'bah. Since then, the custom of changing the Kiswah once a year continues.

## Hatīm

On the northwest side of the Ka'bah is a semi-circular structure known as Hatīm. It is made of white marble. The floor between the Hatīm and the Ka'bah is also covered with white marble. Long ago, the space between the Hatīm and the Ka'bah was part of the Ka'bah. This means that the Ka'bah was once a rectangular structure.

A few years before Muhammadﷺ became the Rasūl, there was a flood in Makkah. The flood damaged the Ka'bah and the Quraish collected money to rebuild it. However, before they could finish rebuilding the Ka'bah, they used all the money they collected. So they could not include the Hatīm in the Ka'bah. The Hatīm was left out. From that time, the structure of the Ka'bah has remained the same, as the Quraish rebuilt it.

## Maqam-e Ibrāhīm

Discussion about the Ka'bah would not be complete without mentioning the **Maqam-e Ibrāhīm**, or the Station of Ibrāhīm. It is a stone block on which Ibrāhīm (A) stood when he built the Ka'bah. It is located a short distance from the door of the Ka'bah. It is reported that Ibrāhīm (A) offered two rak'at prayers after finishing the construction of Ka'bah. After finishing tawāf, during Hajj and Umrah, Muslims offer two rak'at prayers behind Maqam-e Ibrāhīm.

## The Ka'bah in Rasūlullāh's ﷺ time

In Nabi Muhammad's ﷺ lifetime, the Quraish took care of the Ka'bah. The Quraish were idol worshippers. They allowed the Ka'bah to contain hundreds of idols from Arab tribes, including idols of Jesus and Mary. The Ka'bah was full of idols. When Rasūlullāh ﷺ returned from Madīnah, he liberated Makkah from idol worshipping and destroyed all the idols. The Ka'bah was rededicated as **Baytullāh** or Allāh's House. Rasūlullāh ﷺ established that the Hajj should be a Muslim duty.

## The Ka'bah after Rasūlullāh ﷺ

After Rasūlullāh's ﷺ death, the Ka'bah was destroyed several times by flood, fire, and Muslim rulers. One ruler tore it down and reconstructed it to include the Hatīm. Within ten years, another ruler tore it down and rebuilt it the way the Quraish had built it—with the Hatīm separate from the Ka'bah. From that time on, the Ka'bah remained the same, with the Hatīm left out of the Ka'bah.

Repair work and renovations have been undertaken throughout history. However, the structure remains as the Quraish built it. After the Saudi Arabian Government came to power, the surroundings of the Ka'bah were renovated and expanded several times to accommodate a large number of pilgrims.

1. Who identified the Ka'bah as "my home?"

    A.  Ibrāhīm (A).

    B.  Muhammadﷺ.

    C.  Allāhﷻ.

    D.  The Quraish.

2. Where is the Maqam-e Ibrāhīm located?

    A.  Inside the Ka'bah building.

    B.  On the outskirts of Makkah.

    C.  On top of a mountain in Makkah.

    D.  A short distance from the door of the Ka'bah.

3. Who took care of the Ka'bah during Nabi Muhammad'sﷺ lifetime?

    A.  The Yemeni People.

    B.  The Quraish.

    C.  Abdul Muttalib.

    D.  The Ansārs.

4. In which corner of the Ka'bah do we find the Black Stone?

    A.  The Western Corner.

    B.  The Eastern Corner.

    C.  The Southern Corner.

    D.  The Northern Corner.

5. What is a Kiswah?

_____

_____

6. What is the shape of the Hatīm?

    A. Oval.

    B. Circular.

    C. Square.

    D. Semi-circular.

7. When the Ka'bah was re-built by the Quraish, why was the Hatīm kept separate from the Ka'bah?

    A. Rasūlullahﷺ told them to leave it out.

    B. The Quraish did not have enough money to finish construction.

    C. Ibrāhīm (A) told them to leave it out.

    D. The Arabs were fighting, so they did not include it.

8. What does the word "Baytullāh" mean?

    A. Allāh'sﷻ House.

    B. Allāh'sﷻ mercy.

    C. Allāh'sﷻ city.

    D. Allāh'sﷻ tower.

# Masjid an-Nabawī: *The Nabi's Masjid*

**Objective of the Lesson:**

The Masjid an-Nabawī, also known as the Prophet's Mosque, was originally built by Nabi Muhammadﷺ. It was the residence of Nabi Muhammadﷺ, a masjid for early Muslims, and later the grave of Nabi Muhammadﷺ. The history of its early construction is as fascinating, as the history of its future renovations and modifications. Students will learn the basic details about the masjid and its identifying features.

The second-most important masjid in Arabia is the masjid in Madīnah. The most important one is the Great Masjid around the Ka'bah in Makkah. Both of these masajid are also known as **Masjid al-Haram** because hunting or fighting within their boundaries is harām, or prohibited.

The masjid in Madīnah is known as the Prophet's Mosque, or **Masjid an-Nabawī**. This masjid was originally built by Nabi Muhammadﷺ. Like the masjid in Makkah, this masjid was also renovated and expanded several times since its construction. The Masjid an-Nabawī is the second-holiest site in Islam. The holiest site is the Great Masjid in Makkah. Today, the Masjid an-Nabawī is recognized as one of the largest masajid in the world. It is estimated that 1.6 million people can pray in the masjid at any given time.

There is an interesting story about how the location of the masjid was decided. After hijrat, as Rasūlullāhﷺ arrived in Madīnah, everybody wanted him to stay at their house. If Rasūlullāhﷺ had chosen one house, it could have become a source of pride and honor for the family. But other people might have been offended by not being chosen.

Rasūlullāhﷺ told the people to release the rein of his camel and allow her to roam on her own. Wherever she sat would be Rasūlullāh'sﷺ residence. Everyone followed the camel with great enthusiasm. Finally, she stopped near Abū Ayyūb's house. This home became Rasūlullāh'sﷺ lodging for the first few weeks.

Opposite Abū Ayyūb's house, there was an open area used for keeping camels and drying dates. Rasūlullāhﷺ inquired about the area's owner. Someone told him that the land belonged to two orphan boys, named Sahl and Suhail. The two boys were asked to sell the land to Rasūlullāhﷺ at a suitable price. The boys refused to accept any price for the land and offered it free of charge. But Rasūlullāhﷺ would not accept the land without paying for it. Ultimately, with the help of the boys' guardians, a suitable price was agreed upon for the plot of land.

## Rasūlullāh's ﷺ house

Rasūlullāh ﷺ called upon his companions to help him construct his residence and a masjid. The masjid included a large prayer area. Rasūlullāh ﷺ, himself, worked hard on the construction project.

The building was a humble construction in all respects. The walls of the masjid were made of unburned bricks. The ceiling was made of palm leaves placed over supporting frames. It was good enough to prevent the harsh rays of the sun, but not good enough to prevent occasional rainwater from falling inside. No special flooring or carpeting was used. There were a few mats laid down, but most of the companions prayed on a bare, sandy floor. The qiblah was made to face Jerusalem because Muslims faced this direction for their salāt.

Adjacent to the masjid, the companions and Rasūlullāh ﷺ built two rooms as a home for Rasūlullāh ﷺ. During Rasūlullāh's ﷺ lifetime, the masjid was enlarged only once to accommodate more people.

## Other early expansions

During the rule of Abu Bakr (R), the first khalifah, no work was done on the masjid. During the rule of the second khalifah, Umar (R), the masjid was expanded to accommodate more people. Umar (R) demolished all the houses around the masjid except for the houses of the widows of Rasūlullāh ﷺ. He expanded the masjid and almost doubled its original size. The third khalifah, Uthmān (R) demolished the mosque to nearly double its size again.

## Renovations after the khalifas

About 75 years after the death of Nabi Muhammad ﷺ, more renovations took place. By then the rule of four khalifahs had ended. New Muslim rulers rose to power in Arabia. Muslim population increased, necessitating more space in the masjid to pray. One of the rulers renovated the masjid over a period of three years. He almost doubled the size that Uthmān (R) had built. For the first time, minarets were built on the masjid.

## Rawdah

Rasūlullāh died in his wife 'Ā'ishah's (ra) room. He was buried below the place where he had died. This means that he was buried in a grave dug in the floor of 'Ā'ishah's room, below the bed where he had taken his last breath.

A certain area around his grave is called **Rawdah**. The word rawdah means "garden." It is called a garden because the grave and its adjacent area are considered "the garden of paradise."

The rawdah includes two other graves beside the graves of Rasūlullāh. These two graves are those of two Khalifah, Abu Bakr (R) and 'Umar (R).

## Green dome of the masjid

In order to identify the location of the rawdah, a dome was constructed on top of the building. The dome is a more recent construction. It was built by a Muslim empire about 200 years ago. At one time the dome was painted white. Then at a later time, it was painted purple. Finally, it was painted green (see picture).

### Points to Remember

1. Masjid an-Nabawī was built by Nabi Muhammad.

2. The original Masjid did not have a roof.

3. The first expansion of the Masjid was done by Umar ibn Khattab.

4. Jannat al-Baqi is adjacent to the Masjid.

5. At present the Masjid has capacity to hold 2 million people.

## Jannat al-Baqi

Adjacent to the masjid is **Jannat al-Baqi**. This means "Garden of Heaven." It is the main cemetery in Madīnah. A large number of Rasūlullāh's immediate family and companions are buried here.

During Rasūlullāh's lifetime, the cemetery was located outside the city of Madīnah. The city was very small then. The masjid has expanded so many times that the area around the masjid and the Jannat al-Baqi are now next to each other.

In the past, people built domes and other identifying structures on different graves in Jannat al-Baqi. About 100 years ago, the Saudi Arabian government demolished all the domes and other structures and leveled the ground. This was done mainly to prevent people from seeking help from the dead and worshipping the graves.

## Current size of the masjid

After the Saudi government rose to power, it made extensive renovations to the masjid. The masjid was enlarged more than 100 times its original size. When electricity was introduced to entire Arabia, Madīnah was the first city to receive electric lights in 1909.

Major expansions were completed in 1974, 1985, 1992, and 2012. Now 250 large umbrellas have been set up in the courtyard of the masjid. These umbrellas are so large that 800 people can pray under the shade of one umbrella.

With all these expansions and renovations, the masjid can now accommodate about 2 million people to offer their prayer at any given time.

## from Hadīth

Anas ibn Malik narrated that Rasūlullāhﷺ said: " Madīnah is a sanctuary from that place to that. Its trees should not be cut, and no heresy should be innovated nor any sin should be committed in it."

1. Who originally built the Masjid an-Nabawī.

    A. Abū Bakr (R).

    B. Nabi Muhammadﷺ.

    C. Ibrāhīm (A).

    D. The Quraish.

2. What is Jannat al-Baqi?

    A. A cemetery inside the Masjid.

    B. A cemetery of the companions and Rasūlullāh'sﷺ family members.

    C. A door on the eastern wall of the Masjid.

    D. A garden of date trees.

3. What is inside the Rawdah in the Masjid an-Nabawi?

    A. A secret fountain of water.

    B. A footprint of Ibrāhīm (A).

    C. The grave of Nabi Muhammadﷺ.

    D. The grave of 'Ā'ishah (ra).

4. From whom did Rasūlullāhﷺ buy the land on which his house was built?

    A. From the chief of Madīnah.

    B. From the Jews of Madīnah.

    C. From Abū Bakr (R).

    D. From two orphan boys.

5. What does the green dome on Masjid an-Nabawī indicate?

   A. The direction of the qiblah.
   B. The burial ground of the companions Rasūlullāh'sﷺ family members.
   C. The burial place of Nabi Muhammadﷺ.
   D. The location of the Zamzam fountain.

6. When were the minarets in the Masjid an-Nabawī built?

   A. During Abū Bakr's (R) lifetime.
   B. During 'Umar's (R) lifetime.
   C. About 75 years after Rasūlullāh'sﷺ death.
   D. About 200 years earlier from today.

7. About how many people can pray in Masjid an-Nabawī today at one time?

   A. 100,000 people.
   B. 1.6 million people.
   C. 3 million people.
   D. 25 million people.

# Bilāl ibn Rabāh (R)

## Objective of the Lesson:

In this lesson, students will learn about Bilāl ibn Rabāh (R)—a black slave and one of the first to accept Islam. He was not forced to accept Islam, but from the little he heard about it, he believed it was a true religion. His uncompromising dedication to Islam is impressive. His life and sacrifices highlight the overall situation in Arabia and the challenges faced by early Muslims.

The first few years after Rasūlullāh received divine revelation, very few people knew about Islam. Rasūlullāh did not teach the message to everyone. He kept it a secret, telling only his own family and a few close friends. Three years later, Allāh asked Rasūlullāh to discuss Islam openly and invite people to accept Islam. Rasūlullāh called people to make Islam a way of life, submit to one God, and asked worship only Allāh.

People in Makkah were shocked. They were asked to give up all their idols and, instead, worship one God—Allāh. People were asked to change their social and cultural practices. They were asked to change the way they conducted business and to change the way they treated orphans, women, and the poor. People realized

### Points to Remember

This and the next chapter has the names of several companions of our Nabi Muhammad. We should remember to add the prayer "Radi-allāhu 'an-hu" for a khalīfah or a male companion of Rasūlullāh. For a female companion, the prayer "Radi-allāhu 'an-hā" should be used.

Even if it is not mentioned by (R) or (ra), we should show respect by saying the prayer.

that Islam would not only change the way they worshipped, but also it would change the way they lived.

The people in Makkah, particularly the wealthy and powerful ones, realized they had to stop the teachings of Islam. They had to oppose Islam in the strongest way. They had to stop anyone who might become interested in Islam. If they did not do these things, then entire Arabia would be influenced by Islam. So the wealthy and powerful people began to oppose Islam. They focused their opposition particularly on those who had already become Muslim.

## Tribal protection

There was a system of protection in Arabia. If a member of a certain tribe was in danger, the entire tribe would protect the person. This meant that people from one tribe usually would not harm a person from another tribe.

The early Muslims belonged to several different tribes. So, a tribe would not physically harm a member of another tribe, even if he was a Muslim. But this did not prevent people from terrorizing the early Muslims. People began to ridicule and disrespect the Muslims. They began to make life miserable for the Muslims.

## Condition of weak people

The powerless people in the society were slaves and servants. They were at the greatest risk of harm because they did not have any tribal protection. Their master could treat them in a harsh manner. One of these slaves was Bilāl ibn Rabāh (R).

## Bilāl (R) accepts Islam

Bilāl (R) was a black person, and his parents were slaves. As a result, he was also a slave. His master was Umayyah ibn Khalaf. Bilāl worked hard to make his master happy but after days of hard work, he only received a few dates. He often served food to guests in his master's house, but he would not be allowed to eat. Umayyah was a ruthless master, and he treated his slaves very poorly. Umayyah was an idol worshipper. He strongly opposed Islam and Nabi Muhammadﷺ.

Bilāl (R) heard his master and others talking angrily about a person named Muhammadﷺ. Even though they hated Muhammadﷺ, they respected his honesty and kind nature. After hearing such discussions, Bilāl secretly became interested in Islam.

Bilāl (R) found out what he could about Islam, and he believed it was a good religion. He learned that Islam speaks of one God, supports equality of people, assures reward for good work and punishment for bad actions. He heard that God is merciful. After learning these, Bilāl accepted Islam.

## Inhumane torture

Umayyah ibn Khalaf was upset when he learned that his slave had accepted Islam. He joined other Makkan leaders in terrorizing the new Muslims. He wanted to keep the Makkans from even thinking about becoming Muslim.

Umayyah began torturing Bilāl (R) to force him to give up Islam. He brought Bilāl (R) to the open desert, day after day, and severely beat him. In the middle of the day, when the sun was the hottest, Umayyah made Bilāl lie down on the sand without any clothes on to protect him from the burning-hot sand. Then he placed a large boulder on Bilāl's chest to increase his suffering. He tied up Bilāl (R) and dragged him along the hot sand. During these acts of torture, Umayyah asked Bilāl (R) to give up Islam and believe in the idols. Every time, Bilāl (R) answered, "One! One!," meaning God is One.

## Bilāl's release

Such inhumane torture scared many Makkans away from accepting Islam. This torture sometimes lasted for several days. One day, Abū Bakr (R) saw Bilāl (R) being tortured. Abū Bakr (R) tried to intervene, but he failed. Umayyah blamed Abū Bakr (R) that because of people like him, Bilāl (R) dared to become a Muslim. Then he challenged Abū Bakr (R) to save Bilāl by buying him. Abū Bakr accepted the challenge to buy Bilāl. Angry Umayyah offered to sell Bilāl at a low price to indicate Bilāl was not worth very much. Abū Bakr agreed and bought Bilāl. Now Bilāl was Abū Bakr's slave. Immediately after buying Bilāl, Abū Bakr set him free. Bilāl became a free man.

## First muezzin

After Muslims migrated to Madīnah, the adhān practice was established. Rasūlullāhﷺ asked Bilāl (R) to announce the adhān. Thus, he became the first **muezzin**, that is, the person who announces adhān. Bilāl had a beautiful and loud voice. His adhān call filled the sky of Madīnah.

Years later, Rasūlullāhﷺ returned to Makkah. At that time, the Ka'bah contained many idols. Rasūlullāhﷺ destroyed all the idols in and around the Ka'bah. Then he asked Bilāl (R) to make the adhān. Bilāl climbed on the roof of the Ka'bah and announced the adhān.

## Final years

In the history of Islam, Bilāl (R) is remembered as a strong-willed person who did not give up his religion despite extreme punishment. He stood by his faith that Allāh﷽ is the only God. During the rule of Abū Bakr, Bilāl moved to Syria. He remained in Syria for the rest of his life. He died in the city of Aleppo at the age of 64.

## from Hadīth

Regarding repetition of adhān phrases twice and saying the iqamah phrase once, Anas ibn Malik narrated: "Rasūlullāhﷺ commanded Bilāl to repeat the phrases twice in Adhān and once in Iqama."

1. Who was Bilāl ibn Rabāh's (R) master?

    A. Abū Sufyān.

    B. Uthman ibn Affān.

    C. Umayyah ibn Khalaf.

    D. Zaid ibn Hāritha.

2. What was the religious belief of Bilāl's (R) master?

    A. Islam.

    B. Christianity.

    C. Buddhism.

    D. Idol worshipping.

3. When Bilāl's master tortured him in the desert, what was Bilāl's (R) reply?

    A. One! One!

    B. One! Two! Three! Four!

    C. Baitullāh!

    D. Barakallāh!

4. Who rescued Bilāl (R) when he was being tortured?

    A. Nabi Muhammad ﷺ.

    B. 'Uthmān (R).

    C. Abū Bakr (R).

    D. The women in Makkah.

5. Where was the first adhān announced?

    A. In Makkah.

    B. During the first Hajj.

    C. In Madīnah.

    D. On a battlefield.

6. Who was the first muezzin?

    A. Ibrāhīm (A).

    B. Abū Bakr (R)

    C. Nabi Muhammad ﷺ.

    D. Bilāl (R).

7. In which city did Bilāl (R) die?

    A. Damascus.

    B. Madīnah.

    C. Aleppo.

    D. Baghdad.

# Zayd ibn Hārithah (R)

## Objective of the Lesson:

One of the distinguished companions of Rasūlullāhﷺ was Zayd Ibn Hārithah (R). For many years he was known as Rasūlullāh'sﷺ adopted son. This chapter narrates the early life of Zayd (R), focusing on how he was sold at a slave market, and how he became part of Rasūlullāh'sﷺ household. The lesson also describes Rasūlullāh'sﷺ kindness and compassion toward Zayd (R).

Zayd ibn Hārithah (R) was a famous person in the history of Islam. He is the only companion of Rasūlullāhﷺ whose name is mentioned in the Qur'ān. He became famous because so much of what happened to him connected to Rasūlullāhﷺ in one way or another. Therefore, when we study his life, we also get a glimpse of Rasūlullāh'sﷺ life.

## The kidnapping

It is reported that when Zayd (R) was about eight years old, his mother took him on a journey to visit her relatives. Along the way, a group of raiders attacked them, stole their belongings, and kidnapped Zayd (R). The kidnappers sold the boy as a slave in one of the bazaars. A slave boy often did not have much value in the eyes of his master. Zayd (R) was sold a few more times until he ended up in Syria as a slave. Time passed by and Zayd (R) became a young adult.

## A Quraish man buys Zayd

During one of the annual bazaars, a Quraish man traveled to Syria to conduct trade activities. He was Khadījah's (ra) nephew. The Quraish man bought several young slaves and brought them to Makkah. Zayd (R) was one of the slaves brought to Makkah.

This nephew showed Khadījah (ra) the young slaves he brought from Syria. He asked her to take one of the slaves. She chose Zayd (R) and took him home. When Muhammadﷺ saw Zayd (R), he liked the young man right away. He asked Khadījah (ra) to give Zayd to him as a present. Khadījah (ra) happily presented Zayd (R) to her husband. Although Zayd (R) remained in the same household, he now had a new master.

## Freeing of slaves

Not long after Khadījah (ra) offered Zayd (R) to her husband, Muhammadﷺ freed Zayd (R). Freeing a slave meant the slave was no longer under any form of bondage. If the freed slave wanted to leave his or her master, this was allowed.

The condition for most slaves was not good. People treated slaves as unequal to them. But Muhammadﷺ and Khadījah (ra) not only freed their slaves but also cared for them as family members.

## Search for Zayd (R)

After Zayd (R) was kidnapped, his father, Hārithah, searched for him wherever he went. He realized that his son had previously been sold as a slave because the slave trade was common in Arabia.

Zayd's father expressed his sorrow by composing very touching poetry. He recited the poetry in bazaars, hoping that if people liked his poetry, they would memorize it and recite it in other places when they traveled. At that time, poetry was one of the best methods in Arabia

to spread news quickly to distant places. He hoped that wherever Zayd lived, he would hear the poetry and reunite with him.

## Connection established

It just so happened that a traveler went to Makkah and recited a poem composed by Hārithah. When Zayd (R) heard the poem, he realized it was written by his father. So Zayd (R) composed a few lines in which he mentioned that he lived in Makkah. Travelers were amused by the connection. After a period of time, these two poems were spoken in the area where Zayd's father lived. Hārithah was elated to learn where he should look for his missing son—in Makkah.

## Father finds his son

Hārithah and his brother traveled to Makkah to find Zayd (R). Upon their arrival, they learned that Zayd lived in Muhammad's household. They went to Muhammad's house and politely requested that Muhammad allow Zayd (R) to leave.

After hearing their request, Muhammad told them to let Zayd (R) choose. If Zayd (R) chose to go with his father, he would be free to leave. If Zayd (R) chose to live with Muhammad, then he would be allowed to stay. Hārithah and his brother agreed because this idea sounded fair.

Muhammadﷺ summoned Zayd (R) and him two choices: Zayd could leave with his father or he could stay.

Without any hesitation, Zayd (R) said that he would stay with Muhammadﷺ. Hārithah was shocked. He asked why he wanted to remain a slave instead of going back home to his parents. Zayd (R) pointed at Muhammadﷺ and said that he saw special qualities in him and he would never leave him to go anywhere.

## Zayd (R) becomes an adopted son

After Zayd (R) expressed his decision to stay, his father had no choice but to respect his wish. At that point, Muhammadﷺ took Zayd (R) by the hand and they all walked to the Ka'bah. There, in the presence of many people, Muhammadﷺ declared, "Listen, all who are present. Bear witness that this boy is my son. He inherits me and I inherit him." This was the formal method of adoption.

This action by Muhammadﷺ made Hārithah extremely happy. He realized that Zayd (R) was in the best household in all of Arabia. He left Makkah without any regrets in his heart even though he was unable to take his long-lost son home.

For a long time, people continued to call the former slave Zayd ibn Muhammad. Zayd (R) realized that his adoptive father, Muhammadﷺ, had a special love for him. In return, Zayd (R) remained obedient to him during his entire life.

1. How old was Zayd (R) when he was kidnapped?

   A. About 8 years old.
   B. About 15 years old.
   C. About 20 years old.
   D. About 40 years old.

2. What did Khadījah (ra) do with Zayd (R)?

   A. She presented Zayd (R) to her husband.
   B. She sold Zayd (R) to Umayyah ibn Khalaf.
   C. She returned Zayd (R) to his father.
   D. She sold Zayd (R) at another bazaar.

3. What did Zayd's father do to find out where Zayd (R) lived?

   A. He sent spies all over Arabia.
   B. He asked a king to find his son.
   C. He sent secret letters around Arabia.
   D. He composed poetry.

4. What two choices did Nabi Muhammadﷺ give Zayd (R) when Zayd's father came to get him?

   1. _____

   2. _____

5. When did Nabi Muhammadﷺ decide to adopt Zayd (R) as his son?

    A. After Zayd (R) arrived in Madīnah.

    B. After Zayd (R) became sick.

    C. After Zayd (R) decided to stay in Makkah rather than go with his father.

    D. After Khadijah (ra) presented Zayd (R) to Nabi Muhammadﷺ as a slave.

# Unit 6: Akhlaq and Adab in Islam

Throughout the Islamic Studies series, proper Islamic manners and moral issues are emphasized. Good moral conduct does not make a person suffer; it helps one to become better in the sight of humanity and God. Proper akhalq and adab require knowing and demonstrating these concepts and practices in everyday life. Lesson 24 discusses how one can be a good person. Chapter 27 focuses on the value of good deeds and why we should practice good deeds. Kindness, forgiveness, perseverance, and punctuality are some of the qualities present in the lives of great people. Islam teaches us these important values. Our Nabi Muhammad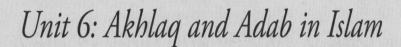 was a living example of these qualities. In this unit, students will learn the importance of good moral values and how to practice them in their daily lives.

**Lesson 24:  How to Be a Good Person**

**Lesson 25:  Kindness:** *A Virtue of the Believers*

**Lesson 26:  Forgiveness:** *A Quality of the Believers*

**Lesson 27:  Good Deeds:** *A Duty of the Believers*

**Lesson 28:  Perseverance:** *Never Give Up*

**Lesson 29:  Punctuality:** *Doing Things on Time*

# Unit 6: Akhlaq and Adab in Islam

## How to Be a Good Person

One of the basic human instincts is to be a good person. All the major religions place importance on being a good person. Islam is no exception. It does not take a lot of effort to be a good person. But it is an ongoing effort to remain one. Students will learn some of the ways they can be good to themselves and to others.

## Kindness: *A Virtue of the Believers*

The teachings of the Qur'ān and the sunnah of Rasūlullāh☀ encourage us to be kind to others. Kindness is positive behavior that everyone can feel and everyone needs. It is a universal language that everyone understands. This chapter explains why being kind to others is a good virtue.

## Forgiveness: *A Quality of the Believers*

Allāh☀ is the most-Forgiving. He will forgive our sins and remove them if we pray to Him. Allāh☀ wants us to have the quality of forgiveness. In this lesson, students will learn the importance of practicing forgiveness.

## Good Deeds: *A Duty of the Believers*

Islam requires us to believe in our faith and prove that we truly believe. Good deeds allow us to prove that we are true believers. Performing good deeds makes us good Muslims. This chapter discusses some good deeds and explains why we should always perform good deeds.

## Perseverance: *Never Give Up*

Islam requires us to show patience and perseverance. Like many other good qualities, perseverance is a quality that can be developed over time with little practice. Students will learn the importance of perseverance as one of the main qualities of true believers.

## Punctuality: *Doing Things on Time*

Timeliness is an important value of Islam. Too often we ignore the responsibility of being timely in our obligations. In this lesson, students will learn why Allāh☀ encourages us to be punctual in life.

# How to Be a Good Person

**Objective of the Lesson:**

One of the basic human instincts is to be a good person. All the major religions place importance on being a good person. Islam is no exception. It does not take a lot of effort to be a good person. But it is an ongoing effort to remain one. Students will learn some of the ways they can be good to themselves and to others.

Learning how to be a good person is a life-long process. A person cannot decide to become a good person in one day. A regular effort is needed to become a good person and remain one throughout life. Sometimes a person is good only for a certain number of months or years. Sometimes the opposite is true.

Many people do not understand the importance of being a good person. Many people think they are good, but they are probably not as good as they think. Some people practice certain good behaviors, but they might not practice other good behavior. For example, a person might be very nice at work, but the same person could be totally different at home—rude, angry, restless, or impatient. In this lesson, we

will learn how to be good people. Let us read what the Qur'ān says about being a good person.

## Qualities of a good person

We can name several qualities that a good person displays in his or her behavior. We can say a good person is someone who is humble, joyful, kind, loving, patient, and respectful. A good person is someone who thinks of others before thinking about himself or herself. A good person is someone who controls his or her anger, never looks down on others, overlooks other's mistakes, forgives, smiles, and helps.

## Why should I be a good person?

We might think that being a good person is boring. We might think there is no fun in being a good person. This is not true. A good person is usually happier and healthier. A good person has peace of mind and is well respected and loved by all. It is in our best interest that we have to be good people. In about 100 verses in the Qur'ān, Allāh says he loves good people and rewards them in this life and in the Hereafter.

*Those who believe and do good, these are the companions of the Garden; in it they abide. (2:82)*

*And those who believe and do good, We shall soon admit them into Gardens beneath which flow the rivers, abiding in it all the time—a promise from Allāh... (4:122)*

*Surely for those who believe and do good, for them are Gardens of Paradise as an entertainment. (18:107)*

*As to those who believe and do good, for them is a reward never to be cut off. (84:25)*

## Begin humble

We can begin to be good in a humble way. To do this, we should realize that we are already good people. We just have to aim a little higher and try a little harder. We are not trying to be perfect, and we are not trying to reach a goal that is too difficult to achieve. We should begin with a reasonable goal. This is the reason we should begin in a humble way.

The best way to begin being a good person is to become humble. How do you do that? First, let go of your pride. The source of your pride could be the house in which you live, the car in which you ride, the clothes you wear, and so forth. Do not allow these things to give you the feeling that you are better than others. The second step is to be kind to others. The third step is to let go of your anger about minor problems.

For example, pretend your brother took your iPad. You want to use it, but he will not give it back. If you are angry about it, let go of your anger. Automatically, you become nice and kind. Automatically, your anger about your iPad subsides. Not having your iPad for an hour or two will not destroy you, and letting go of your anger makes you a better person. You have made a humble beginning. Allāhﷻ loves your behavior because it is humble and kind.

## Let go of anger

Anger is a common emotion. It is important to know that we can control our anger just like we can control other emotions. Of all the emotions, anger can hurt us the most. When we feel angry, we cause damage to our bodies and minds. Therefore, one way to be a good person is to let go of anger.

## Practice forgiveness

When you let go of your anger, you are practicing something noble. You are practicing kindness and forgiveness. We will learn about these two noble virtues—kindness and forgiveness—in the next two lessons. You might have noticed that good people are very forgiving by nature. Our Nabi Muhammadﷺ was a very forgiving person. Let us remember that Allāhﷻ is most-Forgiving, most-Kind. He loves our behavior when we are kind and when we forgive others.

## Be helpful

Another way to be a good person is to help other people. Look for opportunities to be helpful to others. Being helpful is one of the easiest and effective ways to be a good person. But what if someone does not want your help? In that case, respect his or her choice, and politely step back.

## Be polite

Being polite is also an easy way to be a good person. The simple things you do or say can make you become polite. Saying "thank you" or holding a door open for someone are two examples of politeness. Simple politeness such as this can make someone's day. People might not remember your politeness for very long, but this does not matter. People appreciate your politeness right at that moment and that is what matters the most. Whether someone else is rude or impolite should not be your concern. You should always be polite to others.

## Be respectful

A good person respects others. You do not have to like everything about other people, but you should not disrespect them. Everybody is different and everybody thinks and acts differently. All you have to do is simply respect their thoughts and opinions. It is also important to be respectful of your belongings, your school, your masjid, and your country.

## Have patience

One of the greatest qualities of a good person is patience. When things do not go your way, your patience is being tested. Remember the previous example of your brother and your iPad. You were patient when your brother did not return the iPad. Allāh﷾ loves patient behavior. The Qur'ān says that those who are patient ultimately become successful.

*But whoever indeed exercises patience and forgives—that surely is a matter of great determination. (42:43)*

## Be responsible

Another quality of a good person is a sense of responsibility. Children are not responsible for all the things for which adults are responsible. But there are many things for which you are responsible. Placing your dirty clothes in the laundry basket is a simple act of responsibility. Keeping your shoes where they belong is being responsible. Keeping your bedroom neat and tidy is being responsible. After dinner, taking your dishes to the kitchen sink is being responsible. All these responsible actions mean you are also kind, helpful, and respectful.

## Be honest and truthful

A good person is always honest and truthful. With a little practice, you can always be a truthful person. An honest person does not cheat, lie, or steal. Even when no one is watching, you should always do the right thing. You should remember that Allāh﷾ always watches you. Honesty includes what you say and what you do. You should learn to be honest with others and with yourself.

## Adopt the middle path

In all matters in life, we should adopt the middle path. This is our Islamic teaching. A good person will never adopt the extreme path or indulge in an excess of anything.

## Give thanks to Allāh ﷻ

Being a good person means that you are good to your Creator. How do you do that? You become a good person by following Allāh's ﷻ teachings. We often forget to say thank you to our Creator. Allāh ﷻ points out this shortcoming in our behavior.

*Little it is that you give thanks! (7:10)*

Saying "thank you" to people makes us a polite person, and offering thanks to our Creator makes us a humble person.

## For our own sake

Based on this discussion, we have learned that we should be good for our own sake. Do not try to be good only to impress others, or only when your parents tell you to be good. Never act like you are better than others or brag about your "goodness." Remember, we also learned to be polite and humble.

Allāh ﷻ says we are responsible for our own actions. Therefore, we have to be good for our own benefit. If a certain behavior is good for others, then it is good for you as well. When you are a good person, you get the reward, but others receive benefits too.

We all want to be good people in life. We are already good people in many ways. Let us identify one or two areas where we need to work a little harder. Taking another step or two in the direction of self-development will make us better people. May Allāh ﷻ guide us and help us to become better people.

## from Hadīth

'Abdullah bin 'Amr reported that Nabi Muhammad ﷺ said: "A Muslim is the one who avoids harming Muslims with his tongue and hands."

1. Write five things that you can do to be a good person.

1. _____

2. _____

3. _____

4. _____

5. _____

2. Unscramble the following letters to make meaningful words.

**IPLETO**  ☐ ☐ L ☐ ☐ ☐

**GRAEN**  ☐ N ☐ ☐ ☐

**PEHL**  ☐ ☐ ☐ ☐

3. When you let go of your anger, what virtues are you practicing?

1. _____

2. _____

4. What do people often forget to offer Allāh﷾?

    A. Charity.
    B. Thanks.
    C. Share of fruits and meat.
    D. Forgiveness.

5. Which emotion causes the greatest damage to our bodies and minds?

    A. Joy.
    B. Anger.
    C. Sadness.
    D. Happiness.

# Kindness: *A Virtue of the Believers*

**Objective of the Lesson:**

The teachings of the Qur'ān and the sunnah of Rasūlullāh encourage us to be kind to others. Kindness is positive behavior that everyone can feel and everyone needs. It is a universal language that everyone understands. This chapter explains why being kind to others is a good virtue.

Kindness is an important quality for Muslims. Islam teaches us to show kindness to each other and to animals. It is a quality that all Muslims should have. A famous English writer once said, "Kindness is the language which the deaf can hear and the blind can see." This means that kindness is something that everyone can feel and everyone needs. It is a universal language that everyone understands. All the major religions in the world teach people to be kind to others.

It is not only human beings who are kind. Animals can express kindness, and they understand the kindness shown to them. There are many examples available to show animals showing kindness to other animals or to human beings. A dog wags his or her tail in reaction to kindness. Even plants respond to kindness. When you treat a plant with kindness, it grows and bears flowers or fruit in response.

As you can see, an act of kindness never goes to waste. If you are kind, you feel inner peace, and the other person feels happy and thankful. Your act of kindness brings joy to you and the other person.

## Allāh is kind

Allāh is very kind. He is kind to animals, people, and everything else. One of His most beautiful names is **al-Karīm**, which means "the Generous" or "the Kind." Another name, **al-Latīf** means gracious, kind, and affectionate. Two other names, **ar-Rahmān** and **ar-Rahīm**, mean "the most-Kind" and "the most-Rewarding." Allāh is the most-Rewarding because He is the most-Kind.

ٱلْكَرِيمِ        ٱللَّطِيفُ

**al-Karīm**        **al-Latīf**

## How can we be kind?

We might wonder how we can be kind to others. Is being nice to others the same as being kind? Kindness is much more than being nice. Kindness means to bring "action" to being nice.

When you smile at someone you are being nice. If the person is hurt or screaming for help, a simple smile is not enough. You need to take "action." Kindness means helping the person. You can be a nice person and never feed the hungry, never help the poor, never give to charity, or never visit the sick. You become kind only when you take action and start doing good deeds.

The first step to being kind to others is to be nice to others. For example, when you smile at someone, you show that you are friendly and gentle. If you do more than just smile, you show kindness. The examples of Nabi demonstrate that he wanted us to be kind.

1. Kindness is not only being nice, but It is more than that. Explain.

_____ .

2. What does the word al-Latīf mean?

_____ .

We are kind if we speak politely. We should not hurt others with our words. Allāhﷻ tells us to speak politely, even if we are talking to someone who is as bad as Pharaoh.[20:44]

We are kind if we ignore the small faults of others. A simple phrase, such as "Never mind," or "I'll do it" is an act of kindness. The other person will appreciate and remember it.

## Kindness should be your nature

You should not display kindness in certain situations and ignore others. In other words, do not choose when and where to be kind. Kindness should be your nature. Everyone who is near you should feel your kindness. They should not feel like you are arrogant or disrespectful to them. Kindness was the nature of Nabi Muhammadﷺ. Everyone who was near him felt his kindness.

## Rasūlullāh'sﷺ kindness

Rasūlullāhﷺ was a very kind person. We can find many examples of his kindness. He told Muslims to forgive the non-Muslims.[45:14] In fact, many people became Muslim because Nabi Muhammadﷺ was forgiving and gentle in his speech.[3:159] When we forgive people, we make more friends.

One hadīth reports that Rasūlullāhﷺ said, "Be kind to people whether they deserve your kindness or not. If your kindness reaches one who needs it, then it is good for you. If your kindness reaches one who does not need it, then take joy in your kindness."

All the nabis and rasūls were kind. Ibrāhīm (A) was always gentle and forgiving.[11:75] He was kind to his father, even though his father opposed him. Yūsuf (A) was kind to his step-brothers, who treated him terribly.[12:92] Nabi Yahyā (A) was very kind and treated his parents well.

## Be kind to yourself

It is equally important that we are kind to ourselves. Sometimes we make mistakes in our lives. We learn by making mistakes. So if you did something bad, do not hurt yourself. You should be kind to yourself. This will make you happy and help you overcome guilt for the mistake you made.

## Kindness and forgiveness

Kindness and forgiveness belong together. When we forgive a person, we should try to forget that he or she made a mistake.[24:22] If we remember the mistake, then we have not truly forgiven him or her. When we are kind and forgiving, Allāh rewards us.[42:40]

1. How is kindness different from being nice?

_____

2. Write the names of three nabis who were kind to others. Use three names mentioned in the lesson.

3. Which nabi was kind to his father, even though his father opposed him?

_____

4. What is the good quality that belongs with kindness?

_____

5. Which nabi was kind to his step-brothers, even though the brothers were mean to him?

_____

6. Unscramble the following letters to make meaningful words.

**CINE**  ☐ ☐ ☐ ☐

6. Find the following words in the word search puzzle:

FORGIVE   KARIM   LATIF   KIND
NICE   ACTION   ALLAH   MISTAKE

| L | Q | D | N | I | K | S | V | D |
|---|---|---|---|---|---|---|---|---|
| E | N | E | S | L | E | A | C | B |
| K | H | F | F | F | C | W | F | J |
| A | L | L | A | H | I | U | H | C |
| T | I | J | I | U | N | N | U | Y |
| S | E | V | I | G | R | O | F | R |
| I | V | Y | P | L | A | T | I | F |
| M | I | F | M | I | R | A | K | F |
| N | O | I | T | C | A | M | M | F |

# Forgiveness: *A Quality of the Believers*

## Objective of the Lesson:

Allāh﷾ is the most-Forgiving. He will forgive our sins and remove them if we pray to Him. Allāh﷾ wants us to have the quality of forgiveness. In this lesson, students will learn the importance of practicing forgiveness.

Faaris snatched a soccer ball from his friend Asif. At first, Asif was sad. Then he became angry. After a while, Asif let go of his anger and forgave Faaris. Forgiveness allows us to let go of bad feelings in our hearts. Forgiveness means we treat someone nicely, even if the person was not nice to us. Forgiveness is a quality that only good people have.

## Is being angry bad?

Are we not supposed to ever be angry? If so, then why did Allāh﷽ give us this emotion? Fear, disappointment, happiness, sadness, and surprise are some of our normal emotions.

Anger is another emotion that Allāh gave us. Feeling angry is a natural and normal response. What is not normal is to allow anger to take over. When anger takes control of us, we lose our sense of right and wrong. We might do something that makes other people angry.

It is fine to get angry sometimes. But we should always control our anger. We should not be very angry at anyone. Allāh loves those who do not become very angry.[3:134] Forgiveness is the best way to let go of anger.[42:37] Forgiveness reduces anger. Forgiveness helps to heal the hurt you feel.

## Allāh loves forgiveness

In an earlier grade, we learned about Allāh's forgiveness. We learned two of Allāh's most beautiful names, **al-Ghafūr** and **al-Ghaffār**.

الْغَفُورُ          الْغَفَّار

al-Ghafūr          al-Ghaffār

The name al-Ghafūr means that Allāh completely forgives our sins and faults. The name al-Ghaffār means that Allāh forgives again and again, so we are free from the shame of our sin. Another name, **al-'Afuw**, means that Allāh not only forgives but also totally removes the traces of sin.

## We struggle to forgive others

Sometimes forgiving others seems to be the hardest thing to do. Sometimes it feels like it is impossible to forgive others. But if we think about it, we realize that Allāh always forgives us. Every day we make mistakes knowingly and unknowingly. Allāh is al-Ghafūr, al-Ghaffār, and al-'Afuw, so He forgives our mistakes. So why do we not forgive others?

Forgiveness is a quality that we can develop. We cannot become forgiving people in one day. We need to practice. First, we can practice forgiving smaller acts that make us angry or annoyed. If someone is mean to us, we should not be mean in return. We should tell the person that it is not right to be mean. We do not have to verbally tell the person we have forgiven him or her. The fact that we did not become angry or respond angrily is as if we have forgiven the person.

## Revenge is not fun

We do not forgive others because we want to get even with others. We want to cause similar pain for them that they caused for us. However, revenge often makes the situation worse. The other person might strike back to cause even worse pain. Do you then strike back, too? The cycle of revenge might continue. This will only hurt you and make you sad. Instead of all this pain, you can give yourself a gift—forgiveness.

1. Why do people not forgive others?

_____ .

2. What does the word al-'Afuw mean?

_____ .

## Forgiveness is a gift

Forgiveness is a gift that we can give to ourselves. When we forgive, we reduce the anger and the burden of emotional pain. Forgiveness allows us to remove negative thoughts from our minds and direct our energy toward something that makes us happy. On the other hand, if we allow bad feelings to remain in our minds, then we are only hurting ourselves. The person who was mean to us probably no longer thinks about it, but we continue to suffer. When we forgive, we no longer suffer.

## Rasūlullāh's ﷺ example

Allāh ﷻ tells us that Rasūlullāh ﷺ is our best example. We should follow his example in our lives. Let us find out how Rasūlullāh ﷺ responded when people were mean to him.

Once Rasūlullāhﷺ went to a town named **Ta'if** to teach the message of Islam. The people did not want to listen to him. They mistreated him, abused him, and even threw stones at him. He ran away from Ta'if, hurt and bleeding. When he took shelter under a tree, Angel Jibril appeared to him and told him that if Rasūlullāhﷺ wanted, he would destroy Ta'if. Rasūlullāhﷺ chose to forgive the people. He prayed to Allāhﷻ to save the people of Ta'if because they did not realize what they were doing. Years later, the people of Ta'if became Muslim.

## The Makkan people

A long time ago, the Makkan people were enemies of Rasūlullāhﷺ. They fought many battles against him and they wanted to kill him. When Rasūlullāhﷺ liberated Makkah, he could have easily punished his enemies. But he simply forgave everybody. People were very happy about this act of forgiveness. They cried with joy and felt relieved. Many people accepted Islam immediately. Soon, everyone in and around Makkah began to accept Islam. The power of forgiveness is much greater than the power of revenge.

## Nabi Yūsuf's (A) example

When we read about the past nabis and rasūls, we find that they were forgiving too. We learned about nabi Yūsuf (A) in a previous grade. When nabi Yūsuf (A) was a child, his brothers wanted to kill him. They dropped him in a well to die. It was Allāh'sﷻ mercy that saved him. Some travelers rescued him from the well and brought him to Egypt. Yūsuf (A) became an important person in Egypt.

Years later, the brothers went to Egypt for food. Did Yūsuf (A) take revenge on them? No. He forgave them.

## Learn to forgive

You should remember that forgiveness does not happen on its own. You must choose to forgive. When you choose to forgive, you choose to live in the present time instead of remembering the past. When

Rasūlullāhﷺ forgave the people of Ta'if, he chose to live in the present time and forget the past. We should learn from this example of forgiveness. Even if another person causes great harm to us, we should be able to forgive him or her.

When we forgive someone, we should try to forget that he or she made a mistake.[24:22] If we keep thinking about the mistake, then we have not truly forgiven the person. When we are kind and forgive others who hurt us, Allāh﷾ rewards us.[42:40]

Sometimes we make mistakes. When you say **Astaghfirul-Ilāh**, you are seeking Allāh's﷾ forgiveness. Astaghfirul-llāh means "I ask forgiveness from Allāh."

1.  What does forgiveness mean?

_____

_____

2. One of Allāh's﷾ most-Beautiful names means He not only forgives but also totally removes the traces of sin. What is that name?

_____

3. Find an English translation of the Qur'ān. Look up sūrah 9. What is the title of this sūrah?

_____

4. Which sin will Allāh﷾ never forgive?

_____

5. When you say, "Astaghfirul-llāh," what do you seek?

_____

6. Circle **T** if the sentence is true. Circle **F** if the sentence is false

| | | |
|---|---|---|
| Many people became Muslims because Rasūlullāhﷺ was a kind person. | **T** | **F** |
| After we make tawbah, it is fine to do the same bad thing again and again. | **T** | **F** |
| Nabi Muhammadﷺ wanted Angel Jibril to destroy the town of Ta'if because the people of the town had hurt him. | **T** | **F** |

7. What did Rasūlullāhﷺ do with the enemies after he conquered Makkah?

    A. He punished them.

    B. He made them slaves.

    C. He forgave them.

    D. He sent them to another country.

8. Which of the following sentence is correct?

    A. The power of forgiveness is more than the power of revenge.

    B. Revenge is always better than forgiving a person.

    C. Nabi Muhammadﷺ did not forgive the people of Taif.

    D. Forgiveness is a quality of weak people.

9. Forgiveness helps us get over one emotion. What is that emotion?

    A. Fear.

    B. Anger.

    C. Love.

    D. Sadness.

# Good Deeds: *A Duty of the Believers*

**Objective of the Lesson:**

Islam requires us to believe in our faith and prove that we truly believe. Good deeds allow us to prove that we are true believers. Performing good deeds makes us good Muslims. This chapter discusses some good deeds and explains why we should always perform good deeds.

In a previous lesson, we learned some of the ways to be a good person. The activities of a good person become the person's "deeds." The meaning of the word "deed" is action or **conduct**. A good deed means good action or good conduct. We might think good deeds are performed only by good people. But a person who is not usually good can also perform good deeds.

## Islam on good deeds

Islam always encourages performing good deeds. The Qur'ān mentions many good deeds by name. For example, zakāt is a good deed, **sadaqah** or charity is a good deed, and respecting your parents is a good deed. Even knocking on the door before entering someone's house is a good deed. Speaking in a gentle voice is also a good deed.

The Qur'ān says that those who believe and do good deeds will go to heaven.[16:30] If we do not perform any good deeds, we will not receive any rewards from Allāh.

*Surely as to those who believe and do good deeds, for them there is reward without ending. (Surah Fussilat 41:8)*

People perform good deeds for a wide variety of reasons. Most people do not expect a reward in return. When we volunteer to help at school, we do not expect to be paid. But Allāh sees our good deeds. He does not let our good deeds go to waste. This means that He will reward us plentifully for our good deeds.

If we develop some good habits, as discussed in the previous lessons, chances are that most of our deeds will be good deeds.

## Believe and proof of belief

Islam requires us to believe and prove that we truly believe. Performing good deeds proves that we are true believers. On the Day of Judgment, our good deeds and bad actions will be weighed on a **balance**.[7:8] If the load of good deeds is heavy, then we will receive rewards from Allāh. If the load of good deeds is light, then we will suffer. The more good deeds we do, the bigger our rewards will be. Sometimes our minds tell us to do something bad. Not doing this bad thing is also a good deed. Therefore, if we stop doing bad things, our load of good deeds increases. Doing one good deed will not be enough. Doing good deeds once a week or once a month will not be enough. We have to perform good deeds on a regular basis.

1. Write three examples of good deeds.

_____  _____  _____ .

2. Write a good deed that you performed this month.

_____ .

## Shaitān's plan

Shaitān discourages us from doing good deeds. He tries to make us believe that being bad is fun and good deeds are boring. Shaitān is our enemy.[17:53] If we listen to him, we will invite trouble into our lives.

## Example from Madīnah

When Muslims first moved to Madīnah, many people were nice to them. These good people of Madīnah were known as the **Ansars**, or "the helpers." They gave food and housing to the Muslims from Makkah. They also made sure the Muslims were safe in Madīnah. The Muslims were also nice to the Ansars. Muslims taught the Ansars how to practice Islam, and they worked with the Ansars to keep Madīnah safe.

1. What will be used to weigh our good deeds on the Day of Judgment?

_____ .

2. If our load of deeds on the balance is heavy, what will happen to us?

_____ .

## Types of good deeds

Some good deeds are done for others, and some are done for ourselves. Doing well for ourselves means that we do things that benefit us. Taking a shower, trimming our nails, and practicing good **hygiene** are examples of doing well for ourselves. Studying for a test is a good deed. Making salāt is a good deed. Similarly, when we fast, we do it for our own good.

We should also do nice things for others. Before we take any action, we should ask ourselves if our action will hurt someone or damage something. Zakāt and sadaqah are given to needy people to help them. This is an example of doing a good deed for others. We should also be nice to our neighbors, our community, and our nation. We should also be nice to the **environment** and to the animals.

## Good deeds of nabi and rasūl

All the nabis and rasūls performed good deeds throughout their lives. Our Nabi Muhammadﷺ always performed good deeds. A woman often threw trash in his backyard. Nabi Muhammadﷺ cleaned up the trash without complaining. What Nabi Muhammadﷺ did was a good deed, but what the other person did was a bad action.

## Many chances for good deeds

Every day offers new chances to perform good deeds. Helping your parents with chores is a good deed. Keeping your classroom clean is a good deed. Feeding your pets is also a good deed. Not doing something bad is also a good deed. Not talking loudly in class or in the masjid is a good deed. We receive many rewards for our good deeds, so we should try to do good deeds every day.

## fromHadīth

'A'ishah (ra) reported that Nabi Muhammadﷺ said: "Verily, the most complete of believers in faith are those with the best character and who are most kind to their families."

1. On the Day of Judgment, what will be used to measure our good deeds and bad actions?

_____

2. Write three examples of good deeds that you performed last week.

1. _____

_____

2. _____

_____

3. _____

_____

3. As Muslims, we perform many good deeds to help others. Write two deeds that Muslims perform to help others.

_____

_____

4. Unscramble the following letters to make meaningful words.

**KZATA** ☐ ☐ ☐ ☐ ☐

**EDESD** ☐ ☐ ☐ ☐ ☐

**GYEEIHN** ☐ ☐ **G** ☐ **N** ☐

5. Who whispers in our mind not to do good deeds?

_____

6. Give two examples of doing good to our own body.

A. _____

B. _____

7. How often do you think you should do a good deed?

    A.  Once a month.

    B.  Once a year.

    C.  Once during Ramadan.

    D. At all times.

8. What will happen to people who believe and do good deeds?

    A.  They will go to paradise.

    B.  Nobody will help them in the Hereafter.

    C.  They will suffer punishment.

    D. They will be sent back to the earth.

# Perseverance: *Never Give Up*

**Objective of the Lesson:**

Islam requires us to show patience and perseverance. Like many other good qualities, perseverance is a quality that can be developed over time with little practice. Students will learn the importance of perseverance as one of the main qualities of true believers.

When you are really hungry and you have to wait for your mom to finish making dinner, you are showing **patience**. Patience is your ability to accept or tolerate delay without becoming upset or angry. There is another word we often hear that is similar to patience. This word is **perseverance**. It means to continue doing difficult or long work until you are finished.

Not everyone has perseverance, but everyone must possess this quality to be successful in life. Like many other good qualities, perseverance is something that you can develop with a little practice. In order to develop this quality, you need to have strong **determination**.

## Determination

Determination means having a strong intention to finish something or make something happen. It is a God-given gift that we all have been given. However, if we do not use it, eventually we lose it.

For example, when a child learns how to stand up and begins to walk, he or she falls down again and again. Failure does not stop the child. God has given him or her the determination to get up and try again and again. Ultimately, the child learns to walk. The child does not know about determination or perseverance. The child is simply determined to walk and with perseverance, the child learns to walk.

A person who has determination also has self-confidence and a willingness to do hard work. He or she has the energy to continue until the end. This person does not grumble, complain, or become uninterested.

## Two types of sabr

Perseverance means that you do not give up until you finish something or make something happen. In Arabic, this is called **sabr**. There are two kinds of sabr:

1. patience
2. perseverance

Sometimes these words are used to mean the same thing. However, they mean different things. One type of sabr means to wait for a difficult or bad situation to become better. This type of sabr is **patience**. Another type of sabr means to work hard to change a difficult situation. This type of sabr is **perseverance**.

For example, when winter arrives you must have sabr until the cold weather ends. You cannot do anything to make the spring season arrive earlier. You are being patient. But when you need to improve your grades in school, you cannot be idle—you must have perseverance in studying.

If you want to learn how to ride a bike, you will need sabr. You may fall down a few times at first. But if you do not give up, you will soon learn how to ride. You will learn how to ride your bike because you have sabr.

## Give up or try again?

Aminah and Asmah are two friends. They tried to memorize a sūrah together. Aminah gave up after five minutes. Asmah kept on trying. She mixed up a few words in the beginning. She forgot one ayah. But even then she did not give up. She kept practicing. Within a few hours, Asmah memorized the entire sūrah. She had sabr to learn the sūrah.

1. What are the two types of sabr?

_____    _____.

2. During difficult times in life, what type of sabr do you need the most?

_____.

## Secret of success

The Qur'ān says that perseverance is the secret of success.[3:200] Many great authors, musicians, sports players, politicians, and scientists became successful because they understood the value of perseverance. Without perseverance, it is impossible to make great achievements in life. Even if a person is not very talented nor highly knowledgeable, he or she still can succeed in life by simply using determination and perseverance.

On the other hand, a person might be intelligent and talented, but idle and unwilling to work hard. This person will not achieve success because he or she is not determined. In this world, all great things are created or achieved through perseverance.

There is a saying that states "Rome was not built in a day." This means that it took many years to build the city of Rome. Rome was built through determination and the perseverance of thousands of people Imām Bukhārī did not collect six volumes of hadīth book in one day. He worked hard for several decades to compile these hadīth. When Rasūlullāhﷺ began teaching Islam, only a few people believed in him and became Muslim. It took 23 years of hard work and perseverance to spread Islam to hundreds of thousands of people.

## The lives of nabis and rasūls

All the nabis and rasūls had difficult work to do. They showed us how to have sabr during difficult times. Their work included telling people about Allāh﷾ and asking people to do good deeds. Many people did not like the nabis and rasūls. But the nabis and rasūls had sabr and they kept on telling people to be good. Allāh﷾ rewarded them for their sabr.

Nabi **Nūh (A)** and **Ayyūb (A)** are great examples of patience and perseverance. When Nūh (A) preached about Islam to his people, most of them rejected the message. They laughed at him. Yet Nūh (A) did not give up.

Nabi Ayyūb (A) had vast farmland, plenty of wealth, many cattle, and a large family. One by one, his farmland, crops, wealth, and family were lost. His health failed. Even then, he did not complain, lose hope, or give up on Allāh﷾. He showed patience, and Allāh﷾ rewarded him for showing patience. Soon he regained his health, wealth, and farmland. He and his wife had more children.

When nabi **Yūsuf (A)** was a little boy, he was raised by a different family in Egypt. Even as a young boy, he worked hard and remained honest. His sabr brought him great rewards. When he became an adult, he was appointed as an important official in Egypt.

## Nabi Muhammadﷺ

Nabi Muhammadﷺ also did not give up on his difficult duty. His duty was to deliver Allāh's﷾ message to the people. But many people did not listen to him. In Makkah, people were so mean to him that he had to leave Makkah and go to Madīnah. While in Madīnah, he was attacked several times. Yet Nabi Muhammadﷺ did not give up. He had sabr and continued delivering Allāh'sﷻ message. Slowly, more and more people started becoming Muslim. Eventually, all the people of Makkah became Muslim!

## Sūrah al-'Asr

There is a short sūrah in the Qur'ān about success. In this sūrah named **Al-'Asr**, Allāhﷻ tells us that people become successful if they have sabr.[103:1-3] Many other verses in the Qur'ān state that those who have sabr will be rewarded beyond their imagination.[39:10] This is Allāh'sﷻ promise and His promises are always true.[30:60]

When we face difficult times in our lives, we should practice patience by saying the following du'a:

$$إِنَّا لِلَّهِ وَإِنَّا إِلَيْهِ رَاجِعُونَ$$

*Innā lillāhi wainnā ilaihi rāji'un.*
*To Allāh we belong, and to Him is our return. (2:156)*

This du'a teaches us that everything we have comes from Allāhﷻ. If He takes something away, then it is His will. We must accept the will of Allāhﷻ.

## fromHadīth

Nabi Muhammadﷺ said: "No one can be given a blessing better and greater than patience."

1.  Circle **T** if the sentence is true. Circle **F** if the sentence is false.

All nabis and rasūls had sabr.                                     **T**    **F**

We should give up on reading if we face difficult words.          **T**    **F**

If a project becomes difficult, we should give up doing it.       **T**    **F**

Sabr is a type of fruit.                                          **T**    **F**

2. What is the name of the short sūrah in the Qur'ān that describes success?

   _____

3.  In which type of sabr do you wait for the difficult situations to end by themselves?

   _____

4.  In which type of sabr do you work hard until the difficulty ends?

   _____

5. Draw a line to match the words in column A to the correct words in column B.

| **Column A** | **Column B** |
| --- | --- |
| Ayyūb (A) | Sabr |
| Yūsuf (A) | Sūrah on success |
| Sabr | Raised in Egypt |
| al-'Asr | Lost wealth |
| Perseverance | Patience |

6. How many nabi and rasūl practiced sabr?

    A. Some of them.

    B. Ten of them

    C. All of them.

    D. Nobody practiced sabr.

7. What did Allāh do to the nabi and rasūl when they showed sabr?

    A. Allāh rewarded them.

    B. Allāh was angry with them.

    C. Allāh punished them.

    D. Allāh told them to go away.

8. From your life give an example when you showed sabr.

    _____

    _____

# Punctuality: *Doing Things on Time*

## Objective of the Lesson:

Timeliness is an important value of Islam. Too often we ignore the responsibility of being timely in our obligations. In this lesson, students will learn why Allāhﷻ encourages us to be punctual in life.

Whenever we do something on time, it means that we are **punctual**. Punctuality means doing things at their appointed time. When we arrive at school on time, we are punctual. If we do not arrive on time, then we are **tardy**, or late. If you asked your friend to come over at 4:00 o'clock to play basketball and he shows up at 4:30, then he is not punctual.

## Value of punctuality

Punctuality is an important characteristic of all successful people. Think about this—we have 24 hours in a day. A punctual person is able to complete all of his or her tasks within this time. A person who is not punctual does not finish his or her work. A student, teacher, businessperson, firefighter, doctor, engineer, and others all have to be punctual in order to be successful in life.

Can you imagine what would happen if a firefighter did not arrive on time, or a doctor did not show up on time for an important surgery?

### Islam teaches punctuality

Islam encourages us to do things on time. Many of our religious duties require us to be punctual.

For example, salāt and fasting have to be done on time. In the Qur'ān, Allāhﷻ tells us to perform salāt on time.[4:103]

*...the salāt is enjoined on the believers at the prescribed times. (Surah An-Nisa 4:103)*

| Fajr | Dhuhr | Asr | Maghrib | 'Isha |

During the month of Ramadan, the time for fasting is decided by the timing of daylight. In the past, people did not have clocks. They calculated the time based on the position of the sun. Allāhﷻ said that fasting should begin very early in the morning at dawn.[2:187]

*...and eat and drink till it is distinct to you—the white thread from the black thread at dawn; then complete your fast till the night appears... (Surah Baqarah 2:187)*

We break our fast when the sun sets. We may not start fasting between mid-day until midnight. Such fasting would not be accepted by Allāhﷻ. Fasting has to be done at its proper time.

## Punctuality and responsibility

Punctuality teaches us to be responsible. We are responsible if we perform salāt at the appropriate time. If we cannot perform salāt on time due to an emergency, then we are allowed to pray as soon as we have time. But we are not allowed to delay our salāt due to ordinary problems or needs. Salāt cannot be missed, even when we are sick or traveling. Therefore, we should not make it a practice to miss salāt and then make it up later. We should plan for salāt by doing wudu ahead of time. We should plan to pray salāt during break times at school. Such planning teaches us responsibility.

The qualities of responsibility and punctuality make us good human beings. Punctuality is not only a duty but also a part of good manners. If you are punctual, you do your homework on time. A punctual student has time for studies and games. He or she finishes games on time and begins his or her studies on time.

## Even nature is punctual

Let us consider nature. Even nature is punctual in its own way. The sun rises on time and sets on time. Can you imagine what would happen if the sun did not rise or set on time?

The four seasons of the year begin and end at their appointed times. If summer did not arrive on time and if winter lingers for months, the world would face major problems. Everything in nature occurs at the proper time. Thus, nature teaches us to be punctual.

## The cost of not being punctual

Hashim is the best runner in the third grade at his school. He might even be better than the best runner in the fourth grade. Hashim has many good qualities, but he is never on time. On the day of the annual sports event, Hashim was confident that he would win the medal for running. The running competition started at 3:00 pm, but Hashim arrived at 4:00 pm. The competition was already over, and someone else won the medal.

Punctuality teaches us many qualities. Name two qualities.

_____  _____.

## Punctuality teaches respect

Punctuality teaches us to do the right thing at the right age. During childhood, we are required to study and complete our school work. We cannot spend our entire childhood only playing and having fun and plan to go to school when we are older.

Punctuality shows others that you care. When someone invites you to their home and you show up on time, it indicates that you care about the person. Punctuality also shows others that you respect them. If you show respect for others, you will also earn respect.

If you are wondering how to be on time, the answer is actually very simple. Plan to arrive early, and leave your house early. Plan to arrive 10 minutes before any event begins.

Fasting lasts from sunset until the next morning.     True / False

Punctuality means doing things at 12 o'clock.     True / False

Many religious duties require us to be punctual.     True / False

1.  Look at a salāt calendar at home. Then write down the five times for each of the salāt for today.

Fajr: _____

Dhuhr: _____

'Asr: _____

Maghrib: _____

'Isha: _____

2. What time is the Jumuah prayer at your masjid?

_____

3. Islam has five pillars. Write two pillars that require us to perform them in a punctual manner.

1. _____

2. _____

4. Unscramble the following letters to make meaningful words.

**DYATR**

**ASATL**

**LALHA**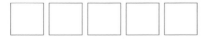

5. Practice of punctuality teaches us many values. Write four values that we learn by being punctual.

A. _____

B. _____

C. _____

D. _____

6. Circle T if the sentence is correct. Circle F if the sentence is false.

| | | |
|---|---|---|
| Islam teaches us to do things on time. | T | F |
| Fasting teaches us the value of being punctual. | T | F |
| If you are very punctual, Allāhﷻ will not reward you. | T | F |
| Nobody will like you if you are punctual. | T | F |

# Appendix

# Steps of Salāt

## Physical preparation for salāh:

**Physical cleanliness:** Before performing salāh, make sure your body is clean. You must complete *wudu*, and be in the state of *wudu*. During the salāh, do not look sideways, do not look at others, and do not talk to others. Do not make unnecessary movements. Do not scratch, yawn, laugh, or smile. If you must sneeze or cough, that is fine, but try to minimize the noise.

**Clean clothes:** Your clothes should be clean and should cover your body. For boys, clothes should cover the body at least from the navel to the knees. For girls, clothes should cover the body from the neck to the ankles, and to the wrists. The head should be covered, but the face can remain uncovered. Clothes should not be transparent. Avoid any clothing that has pictures of people, animals, or offensive writing.

**Clean place:** You should find a clean place to make your salāh. A prayer rug is not necessary. A prayer rug should always be clean, so it ensures a clean place while you are praying.

**Direction to face:** You should face *Qiblah*, which is the direction of the Ka'bah in Makkah.

**Time:** *Fard* (compulsory) prayers are performed at the proper time. It is preferable to perform the prayer as soon as the *Adhān* (call to prayer) is announced.

**Mental preparation:** We begin the prayer with full mental and physical attention. During salāh, we are worshipping and talking directly to Allāh, therefore, we must provide our total attention. Avoid any place or object that diverts your full attention.

**What is a raka'ah?** Each salāh can be divided into cycles of physical postures, or raka'at. Each raka'ah involves the positions of *qiyam* (standing), *ruku* (bowing), *sujud* (prostration), *jalsa* (sitting), another *sujud* (prostration), and associated recitations. The chart shows the specified number of raka'at for the five daily salāh. Some variation in the number of Sunnah prayers exists among the madhhab.

|  | Sunnah raka'at before Fard raka'at | Fard raka'at | Sunnah raka'at after Fard raka'at |
|---|---|---|---|
| **Fajr** | 2 | 2 |  |
| **Dhuhr** | 4 | 4 | 2 |
| **'Asr** | 4 | 4 |  |
| **Maghrib** |  | 3 | 2 |
| **'Isha** | 4 | 4 | 2, then 3 (wajib) |

## Description for a salāh of two raka'at:

The following description of steps is for a salāh with two raka'at (for example, the Fard prayer of Fajr). At the end of this description, there are brief notes about how to perform three or four raka'at of salāh.

### Step 1
(Figures above)

When you stand up for salāh, make an intention to perform the salāh for the sake of Allāh. Say to yourself (in any language) that you intend to offer this *Salāh* (*Fajr, Dhuhr, Asr, Maghrib,* or *Isha*), *Fard, Sunnat,* or *Witr,* and the number of raka'ahs (example—"I intend to offer two *raka'ah* of *Fard, Fajr* prayer for Allāh").

**Position:** *Qiyam.* Stand upright. Raise both hands up to the ears (palms and body facing the direction of the Ka'bah).

**What to say:** *"Allāhu Akbar."* (Allāh is the Greatest).

### Step 2
(Figures on the right)

**Position:** Place your left hand over your belly, place your right hand on top of the left hand, and grip the wrist of the left hand.

**What to say:**

1. *"Subhanaka Allāhumma wa bihamdika, wa tabārakasmuka, wa ta'āla jadduka, wa lā ilāha ghairuka."* (This part is known as *thana.* It means "Glory be to you, O Allāh, and praise to You. Blessed be Your Name, exalted be Your Majesty and Glory. There is no god but You.")

2. *"A'ūdu billāhi mina ash-Shaytānir rajim."* (I seek the protection of Allāh against Shaitān, the condemned.)

3. *"Bismillāhir rahmānir rahīm."* (In the Name of Allāh, Most Gracious, Most Merciful.)

4. Now recite Sūrah Al-Fātihah. We must recite Sūrah Al-Fātihah during each raka'ah. A salāh is not valid if Sūrah Al-Fātihah is not recited.

*"Al humdu li-llahi rabbi-l 'alamīn. Ar-rahmāni-r rahīm. Māliki yawmi-d dīn. Iyyāka na'budu wa iyyāka Nāsta'īn. Ihdina-s sirāta-l mustaqīm. Sirātal ladhīna an'amta 'alaihim, ghairil maghdūbi 'alaihim, wa la-d dāllīn. (Āmīn.)"*

(The Praise belongs to Allāh, The Rabb of all the worlds; the Rahman; the Rahim. Malik of the Day of Judgment. You alone do we serve, and to You alone we seek help. Guide us on the Right Path—the path of those upon whom You have bestowed favors; not of those upon whom wrath is brought down, nor those gone astray.)

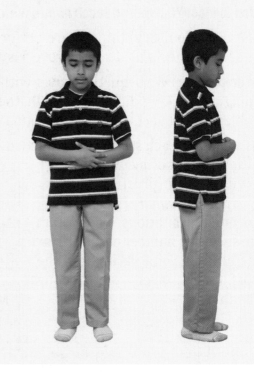

5. After reciting sūrah Fātihah, we now recite any short sūrah or a few verses from the Qur'ān. This additional recitation of part of the Qur'ān is done during the first two raka'ah only. It is always good to memorize as many sūrah as you can, so you can recite them during your salāh.

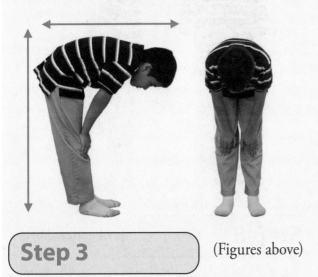

## Step 3 (Figures above)

**What to say:** *"Allāhu Akbar."*

**Position:** This position is called *ruku*. Bow with your back perpendicular to your legs. Place your hands on your knees. Do not bend the knees.

**What to say:** *"Subhana rabbiyal 'Adhīm."* Say this three times. (Glorified is my Rabb, the Great.)

## Step 4 (Figures below)

While going back to the *qiyam* (upright) position,

**What to say:** *"Samia Allāhu liman hamidah."* (Allāh listens to him who praises Him.)

**Position:** In *qiyam* position.

**What to say:** *"Rabbanā wa laka al hamd."* (Our Rabb, praise be for You only.)

## Step 5 (Figure above)

**What to say:** While moving to the next position of *sujud*, say *"Allāhu Akbar."*

**Position:** This position is *sujud*. Place both of your knees on the floor. Try not to move the position of your feet, that is, do not move your feet away from the *qiyam* position. After placing the knees, place your two hands on the floor with palms touching the floor. Do not glide your hands on the floor. Your elbow is not on the floor. Your hands should be sufficiently apart to leave room for your head. Now place your forehead on the floor. Both your nose and forehead should touch the floor. Your hands are on the side of your head. Your stomach will not touch the floor. You should be the most humble in this position.

The most powerful part of our body is our brain, the site of our intelligence. We submit our full selves, with full understanding, to Almighty Allāh. We realize that our strength, power, wealth, and everything that we have is from Allāh. To emphasize this physical and spiritual humility, we will repeat the *sujud* position again in Step 7.

**What to say:** *"Subhana rabbiyal A'ala."* (Say this three times. Glory be to Allāh, the Exalted.)

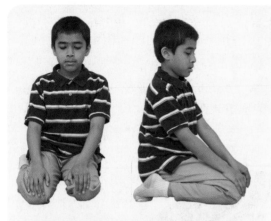

## Step 6
(Figures above)

The next position is *jalsa*.

**What to say:** While moving to the *jalsa* position, say *"Allāhu Akbar."*

**Position:** To move to *jalsa* position, rise from *sujud*. First you will raise your head off the floor, then you will raise your hands. Now you are sitting on the floor— this posture is called *jalsa*.

**What to say:** *"Rabbi-ghfir lī wa rhamnī."* (O my Rabb, forgive me and have mercy on me.)

## Step 7
(Figure above)

We will repeat *sujud* again. Every *raka'ah* has two *sujud*.

**What to say:** While moving to the sujud position, say *"Allāhu Akbar."*

**Position:** *Sujud*. Place your palms on the floor and then your forehead. Both the nose and the forehead should be touching the floor.

**What to say:** *"Subhāna rabbiyal A'ala."* Say this three times. (Glory to Allāh, the Exalted.)

## This completes one raka'ah.

## Step 8
(Figures above)

Rise to the *qiyam* (standing) position. The movement should be in a systematic, graceful manner. First you will raise your forehead from the floor, next you will raise your hands and then you will raise your knees. Try not to move your feet—that is, the position of your feet should be the same as it was during the first raka'ah.

**What to say:** While moving to the qiyam position, say *"Allāhu Akbar."*

**Position:** Stand upright. Hold the left hand with the right hand on top.

**What to say:** Sūrah Al-Fātihah, then any short sūrah or a few verses from the Qur'ān.

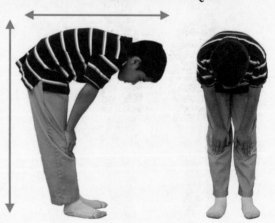

## Step 9

(Figures on the previous page)

**What to say:** *"Allāhu Akbar."*

**Position:** *Ruku.* Bow with your back perpendicular to your legs. Place your hands on your knees.

**What to say:** *"Subhāna rabbiyal 'Adhīm."* Say this three times.

## Step 10

(Figures above)

**Position:** While moving back to the *qiyam* (standing) position,

**What to say:** *"Sami'a Allāhu liman hamidah."*

**Position:** In *qiyam* position. You are upright.

**What to say:** *"Rabbanā wa lakal hamd."*

## Step 11

(Figure below)

**What to say:** While moving to the sujud position, say *"Allāhu Akbar."*

**Position:** *Sujud.* Follow the same sequence as in Step 5.

**What to say:** *"Subhāna Rabbiyal A'ala."* Say this three times.

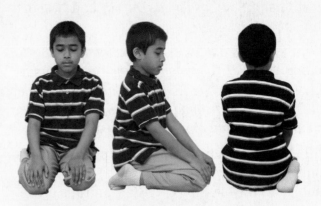

## Step 12

(Figures above)

**What to say:** While moving to the jalsa position, say *"Allāhu Akbar."*

**Position:** Rise from the *sujud* position. Now you are sitting in the *jalsa* position.

**What to say:** *"Rabbi-ghfir lī wa rhamnī"* (O my Rabb, forgive me and have Mercy on me.)

## Step 13

(Figure above)

**What to say:** While moving to the sujud position, say *"Allāhu Akbar."*

**Position:** *Sujud.* First place your hands and then your forehead on the floor.

**What to say:** *"Subhāna Rabbiyal A'ala."* Say this three times.

## Step 14

(Figures in the next page)

**What to say:** While going to the jalsa position, say *"Allāhu Akbar."*

**Position:** Rise from the *sujud* position. Now you are sitting in the *jalsa* position.

**What to say:** Say *Tashahud, Durūd,* and a short prayer as follows:

*"At-tahiyātu lillahi was-salawātu wattaiyibātu. Assalāmu 'alayka ayyuhan-nabiyu wa rahmat-ullāhi wa barakātuhu. Assalāmu 'alainā wa 'ala 'ibadi-llāhis-sālihīn. Ashhadu an lā ilāha illallāhu wa ashhadu anna Muhammadan 'abduhu wa rasūluhu."*

(All these salutations, prayers, and nice comments are for Allāh. Peace be on you, O Prophet, and the blessings of Allāh, and His grace. Peace on us and on all the righteous servants of Allāh. I bear witness that none but Allāh is worthy of worship, and I bear witness that Muhammad is the servant and messenger of Allāh.) This is known as *Tashahud.*

**Position:** Raise your right index finger, so it is pointing upward, while reciting the last part of this prayer.

Next you will recite the *Durūd.*

*"Allāhumma salli 'ala Muhammadin wa 'ala āli Muhummadin, kamā sallayta 'ala Ibrāhima, wa ala āli Ibrāhima, innaka hamidun majid. Allāhumma barik 'ala Muhammadin wa 'ala āli Muhummadin, kama barakta ala Ibrāhima, wa 'ala āli Ibrahīm, innaka hamīdun majīd."*

(O Allāh, send your Mercy on Muhammad and his posterity as you sent Your mercy on Ibrāhīm and his posterity. You are the Most Praised, The Most Glorious. O Allāh, send your Blessings on Muhammad and his posterity as you have blessed Ibrāhīm and his posterity. You are the Most praised, The Most Glorious.)

Now you may add a short prayer, such as:

*"Rabbanā ātinā fi-d dunyā hasanatan wa fi-l ākhirati hasanatan, wa qinā 'adhāban nār."*

(Our Rabb, give us the good of this world, and good in the Hereafter, and save us from the chastisement of Fire.)

**Step 15**　　(Figure above left)

**Position:** Slowly turn your head and face right. This is called *salam.*

**What to say:** *"As-salāmu 'alaikum wa rahma-tullāh."* (Peace and mercy of Allāh be on you.)

**Step 16**　　(Figure above right)

**Position:** Slowly turn your head and face left. This is called *salam.*

**What to say:** *"As-salāmu 'alaikum wa rahma-tullāh."*

## This completes the two raka'at of salāh.

## How to pray three raka'at (Maghrib)

In order to perform a three-raka'at salah, use all the postures and prayers up to step 13.

In step 14, recite up to *"At-tahiyātu lillahi was-salawātu wattaiyibātu. Assalāmu 'alayka ayyuhan-nabiyu wa rahmatullāhi wa barakātuhu. Assalāmu 'alainā wa 'ala 'ibadi-llāhis-sālihīn. Ashhadu an lā ilāha illallāhu wa ashhadu anna Muhammadan 'abduhu wa rasūluhu."* This is known as *Tashahud.*

After saying *"Allāhu akbar,"* return to the *qiyam* position, step 8. This time recite only *Al-Fātihah* (in step 8), but do not recite any sūrah or part of the Qur'ān. All prayers and postures are the same as shown in steps 9–16.

## How to pray four raka'at (Dhuhr, 'Asr, and 'Isha)

In order to perform a four-raka'at salah, use all the postures and prayers up to step 13.

In Step 14, only the *Tashahud* prayer will be recited, and the *qiyam* position, in step 8, will be resumed.

In step 8, only *Al-Fātihah* will be recited without adding any sūrah. Steps 8–13 complete the third raka'ah. The *qiyam* position in step 8 will be resumed.

In step 8, only *Al-Fātihah* will be recited without adding any sūrah. Steps 8–16, complete the fourth raka'ah.

---

**From the Qur'an**

...keep up the salāt, as salāt controls indecent and unacceptable behaviors... *(Sūrah Al-'Ankabūt, 29:45)*

Take care to do your salāt, praying in the best way, and stand before Allāh with full devotion. *(Sūrah Al-Baqarah, 2:238)*

# Summary of Prayer Postures

Standing for salāt facing the direction of the Ka'bah.

Front and lateral view

Raising hands for takbir. Folding them back to recite sūrah.

Bending position for ruku.

Front and lateral view

Rising from ruku.

Performing *sujud*.

Sitting down from the *sujud*, this is *jalsa* position.

Front, lateral and back view

Second *sujud* from the *jalsa* position.

At the end of the second raka'at, sitting down after the second *sujud* to recite *tashahud*.

Completing salāt—turning face first to the right and then to the left.

# Outline of Curriculum – Levels 1, 2 and 3

Each year the curriculum begins with a few topics on Allāh, the Qur'ān, the Nabī, the Hadīth, or Sunnah. In the early years, emphasis is placed on the five-pillars, and each year, this emphasis increases. Every year, a history of some of the messengers is introduced in an age-appropriate manner. Several lessons are devoted to Islamic manners, values, and morals so that children grow up with a good understanding of Islamic culture. Each lesson includes a short homework assignment.

| Level 1 | Level 2 | Level 3 |
|---|---|---|
| **Unit 1: Aqaid: Our Belief** | **Unit 1: The Creator–His Message** | **Unit 1: Knowing About Allah** |
| Allah: Our Creator | Allāh: Our Creator | Who is Allāh? |
| Islam | How Does Allāh Create? | What Allāh Is and Is Not |
| Our Faith | Allāh: What Does He Do? | Allāh: The Most-Merciful |
| Nabi Muhammad | What Does Allāh Not Do | Allāh: The Best Judge |
| The Qur'an | The Qur'ān | What Does Allāh Want Us to Do? |
| **Unit 2: Knowing Allah** | Hadīth and Sunnah | **Unit 2: Teachings of Islam** |
| Allah Loves Us | **Unit 2: Our Ibadat** | We Are Muslims: We Have 'Imān |
| Remembering Allah | Shahadah: The First Pillar | Belief in the Qur'ān |
| Allah Rewards Us | Salāt: The Second Pillar | Belief in the Messengers |
| **Unit 3: Our Ibadat** | Zakāt: The Third Pillar | Hadīth and Sunnah |
| Five Pillars of Islam | Sawm: The Fourth Pillar | Jinn |
| Shahadah: The First Pillar | Hajj: The Fifth Pillar | Muslims in North America |
| Salah: The Second Pillar | Wudū: Keeping Our Bodies Clean | The Straight Path: The Right Path |
| Zakat: The Third Pillar | **Unit 3: Messengers of Allah** | **Unit 3: Life of Nabi Muhammad** |
| Fasting: The Fourth Pillar | Ibrāhīm (A): A Friend of Allah | Kindness of Rasūlullāh |
| Hajj: The Fifth Pillar | Ya'qūb (A) and Yūsuf (A) | How Rasūlullāh Treated Others |
| **Unit 4: Messengers of Allah** | Mūsā (A) and Hārūn (A) | Our Relationship with Rasūlullāh |
| Adam (A): The First Nabi | Yūnus (A) | **Unit 4: Messengers of Allah** |
| Nuh (A): Saved From Flood | Muhammad: Rasūlullāh | Ismā'īl (A) and Ishāq (A) |
| Ibrahim (A): Never Listen to Shaitan | **Unit 4: Learning About Islam** | Shua'ib (A): A Nabi of Allāh |
| Musa (A): Challenging A Bad Ruler | Obey Allāh, Obey Rasūl | Dāwūd (A): A Nabi of Allāh |
| Isa (A): A Great Nabi of Allāh | Day of Judgment and the Hereafter | 'Isā (A): A Nabi of Allāh |
| **Unit 5: Other Basics of Islam** | Our Masjid | **Unit 5: Learning About Islam** |
| Angels: They Always Work for Allāh | Common Islamic Phrases | Ka'bah |
| Shaitan: Our Enemy | Food that We May Eat | Masjid Nabawi |
| Makkah and Madīnah | **Unit 5: Akhlaq and Adab in Islam** | Bilāl ibn Rabāh |
| Eid: Two Festivals | Truthfulness | Zaid ibh Harithah |
| **Unit 6: Akhlaq and Adab in Islam** | Kindness | **Unit 6: Akhlaq and Adab in Islam** |
| Good Manners | Respect | Ways To Be a Good Person |
| Kindness and Sharing | Responsibility | Kindness: A Virtue of the Believers |
| Respect | Obedience | Forgiveness: A Good Quality |
| Forgiveness | Cleanliness | Good Deeds: A Duty of the Believers |
| Thanking Allāh | Honesty | Perseverance: Never Give Up |
| | | Punctuality: Doing Things on Time |

# Outline of Curriculum – Levels 4, 5 and 6

By Level 5, students have learned the biography of the Nabi Muhammadﷺ, including a summary of the events that shaped his life and early Islam. By Level 6, students will have read the biographies of most of the prominent messengers. At this stage, students will have learned all the fundamental principles and key concepts of Islam. Even if students do not attend weekend schools after Level 6, they have already gained significant knowledge about Islam.

| Level 4 | Level 5 | Level 6 |
|---|---|---|
| **Unit 1: Knowing the Creator** | **Unit 1: The Creator, His Message** | **Unit 1: The Creator** |
| Rewards of Allāhﷻ: Everybody Receives Them | Tawhīd, Kāfir, Kufr, Shirk, Nifāq | Attributes of Allāhﷻ |
| Discipline of Allāhﷻ | Why Should We Worship Allāhﷻ? | The Promise of Allāhﷻ |
| Names of Allāhﷻ | Revelation of the Qur'ān | **Unit 2: The Qur'an and Hadīth** |
| Books of Allāhﷻ | Characteristics of the Messengers | Objectives of the Qur'an? |
| **Unit 2: How Islam Changed Arabia** | **Unit 2: The Battles, Developments** | Compilation of the Qur'ān |
| Pre-Islamic Arabia | Pledges of 'Aqabah | Previous scriptures and the Qur'ān |
| The Year of the Elephant | The Battle of Badr | Compilation of Hadīth |
| Early Life of Muhammadﷺ | The Battle of Uhud | **Unit 3: Fundamentals in Deen** |
| Life Before Becoming a Nabi | The Battle of the Trench | Importance of Shahādah |
| First Revelation | The Treaty of Hudaibiyah | Khushū in Salāt |
| Makkah Period | Liberation of Makkah | Taqwā : A Quality of True Believers |
| Hijrat to Madīnah | **Unit 3: The Messengers of Allāh** | **Unit 4: Some Messengers of Allāh** |
| Madīnah Period | Adam (A): The Creation of Mankind | Nūh (A) |
| **Unit 3: The Rightly Guided Khalīfah** | Ibrāhīm (A) Debate with Polytheists | Tālūt, Jālūt, and Dāwūd (A) |
| Abū Bakr: The First Khalifah | Ibrāhīm (A): Plan Against Idols | Dāwūd (A) and Sulaimān (A) |
| 'Umar ibn al-Khattāb | Luqmān (A): A Wise Man's Lifelong Teachings | Mūsā (A) and Fir'awn |
| 'Uthmān ibn 'Affān | Yūsuf (A): His Childhood | Mūsā (A) and Khidir |
| 'Ali ibn Abū Tālib | Yūsuf (A): His Righteousness | 'Isā (A) and Maryam (ra) |
| **Unit 4: The Messengers of Allāh** | Yūsuf (A): Dream Comes True | **Unit 5: Women of Islam** |
| Hūd (A): Struggle to Guide People | Ayyūb (A): Patience, Perseverance | Khadījah (ra) |
| Sālih (A): To Guide the Misguided | Zakariyyāh (A), Yahyā (A) | 'A'ishah (ra) |
| Mūsā (A): His Life and Actions | **Unit 4: Islam in the World** | Fātimah (ra) |
| Sulaimān (A): A Humble King | Major Masājid in the World | Some Prominent Muslimah |
| **Unit 5: Fiqh of Salāt** | **Unit 5: Islamic Values, Teachings** | **Unit 6: Knowledge Enrichment** |
| Preparation for Salāt | Upholding Truth: A Duty for All Believers | Al-Qiyāmah: The Awakening |
| Requirements of Salāt | Responsibility and Punctuality | Rūh and Nafs |
| Mubtilāt us-Salāt | My Mind My Body | The Angels and Jinn |
| How to Pray Behind an Imām | Kindness and Forgiveness | Shaitān: The Invisible Enemy |
| **Unit 6: General Islamic Topics** | The Middle Path: Ways to Avoid Two Extremes | **Unit 7: The Current Society** |
| Compilers of Hadīth | Salāt: Its Significance | My Friend Is Muslim Now |
| Shaitān's Mode of Operation | Sawm: Its Significance | Friendship: With People of Same and Opposite Gender |
| Day of Judgment | Zakāt and Sadaqah: Similarities and Differences | Muslims Around the World |
| Eid: Its Significance | | People of Other Faith |
| Truthfulness: A Quality of Muslim | | **Unit 8: Developing Islamic Values** |
| Perseverance: Keep on Trying | | Greed and Dishonesty |
| | | Avoiding Extravagance |

# Outline of Curriculum – Levels 7, 8 and 9

In these levels, the application of knowledge is increasingly emphasized by offering carefully selected topics. Specific details about some of the messengers are introduced to highlight the abiding morals in their lives. In Level 8, early Muslim struggles are discussed in detail. Increased depth and information in the lessons require focused attention from students. Age-appropriate moral lessons are also covered including gossip, friendship, peer pressure, dating, indecency, encouraging good and forbidding evil.

| Level 7 | Level 8 | Level 9 |
|---|---|---|
| **Unit 1: The Creator** | **Unit 1: Knowing the Creator** | **Unit 1: A Reflection on the Divine** |
| Why Islam? what is Islam? | Divine Names | Signs of Allāh in nature |
| Belief in Allāh | Sunan of Allāh | Pondering the Qur'ān |
| The Qur'ān: Its Qualitative Names | Objectives of the Qur'ān | Preservation and Compilation of the Qur'ān |
| Istighfar: Seeking Forgiveness of Allāh | Sūrah Hujurat: Its Teachings | Ibadat—Easy Ways to Do It |
| Allāh: Angry or Kind | True Piety: Analysis of Verse 2:177 | **Unit 2: An Islamic Perspective** |
| **Unit 2: Stories of the Messengers** | Ayātul Kursi | Why Human Beings Are Superior |
| Ādam (A): Trial of the Messenger | **Unit 2: The Messenger of Allāh** | Is Islam a Violent Religion? |
| Life of Ibrāhīm (A) | The Person Muhammad | Shariah |
| Sacrifice of Ibrāhīm (A) | Farewell Pilgrimage | Justice in Islam |
| Lūt (A): Message for Modern Societies | Finality of Prophethood | **Unit 3: Ethical Standard in Islam** |
| Yūsuf (A)—The Will to Overcome Temptation | Hadīth: Collection, Classification | Peer Pressure |
| **Unit 3: Stories from the Qur'ān** | **Unit 3: Challenges in Madīnah** | Choices We Make |
| Companions of the Cave | Hypocrites | Islamic Perspective on Dating |
| Dhul Qurnain: Journey of a King | Banu Qaynuka | Indecency |
| Effective Debate and Negotiation Styles in the Qur'ān | Banu Nadir | Alcohol and Gambling |
| **Unit 4: Two Companions** | Banu Qurayzah | Permitted and Prohibited Food |
| Abū Sufyān | Mission to Tabūk | Food of the People of the Book |
| Khālid Ibn Walīd (R) | **Unit 4: Islamic Ethical Framework** | Family Values |
| **Unit 5: Knowledge Enrichment** | Friends and Friendship | **Unit 4: Essays on Rasulullah** |
| The Character of the Messengers | Friendship With Non-Muslims | Khadījah (ra) |
| Rasūlullāh's Marriages | Dating in Islam | Rasūlullāh's Multiple Marriages |
| Lailatul Qadr | Golden Rules to Live By | Marriage to Zainab (ra) |
| Fasting During Ramadan | Elements of Bad Life | The Prophet: A Great Army General |
| My Family is Muslim Now | **Unit 5: Islamic Values, Teachings** | Prophecy of Muhammad in the Bible |
| Science in the Qur'ān | Duties Toward Parents | Allegations Against Rasūlullāh |
| Lessons from Past Civilizations | Hope, Hopefulness, Hopelessness | **Unit 5: A Reflection on Islam** |
| **Unit 6: Teachings of the Qur'ān** | Trials in Life | God's Chosen People |
| Amr Bil Ma'rūf | Permitted and Prohibited Food | Mūsā's Personality |
| Guard Your Tongue | Performance of Hajj | Essentials of Salah |
| Islamic Greetings | Parables in the Qur'ān | Life Cycle of Truth |
| How to Achieve Success | **Unit 6: Islam After the Rasul (S)** | How Ramadan Makes Us Better |
| Permitted and Prohibited | Origin and History of Shī'ah | Muslims in North America |
| Types of Behavior Allāh Loves | Ummayad Dynasty | |
| | Abbasid Dynasty | |

# Outline of Curriculum – Levels 10, 11–12

In Level 10 and 11–12, Islamic topics increasingly prepare youths to fine-tune their spiritual and social lives. Significant issues that have real-life implications are introduced. The application of knowledge continues to be emphasized. The lessons in the Level 11–12 book strongly promote the application of Islamic knowledge. This is achieved through carefully selected topics. All lessons teach core Islamic beliefs and understandings based on the Qur'ān and authentic Hadīth.

| Level 10 | Level 11–12 |
|---|---|
| **Unit 1: Knowing the Creator** | **Unit 1: Understanding Our Belief** |
| Understanding the Word "Allāh" | Islam |
| Al-Fātihah: An Analysis of its Message | Muslim |
| Al-Fātihah vs The Lord's Prayer | Shahādah |
| Muhkam and Mutashābihat Āyāt | Belief in Allāh |
| Al-'Asr: The Formula of Success | Belief in the Angels |
| Qur'ānic Calligraphy | Belief in the Revealed Books |
| **Unit 2: Interfaith Studies** | Belief in the Messengers |
| The Bible and the Qur'ān | Belief in the Hereafter |
| The Ten Commandments and Islam | **Unit 2: The "Driver" Within Us** |
| Our Faiths: Key Differences | Life's Ultimate Purpose |
| **Unit 3: Marriage and Family in Islam** | Wealth Is The "Driver" |
| The Status of Women in Islam | The "Driver" Within Us |
| Marriage to Non-Muslims | **Unit 3: A Heart for Allāh** |
| Marrying Four Women | When Allāh Seems Distant |
| Difficult Questions on Marriage | Tawakkul: Trust in Allāh |
| A Muslim Family | Du'ā: How Does Allāh Respond? |
| **Unit 4: General Islamic Topics** | A Heart for Allāh |
| Who are the Khalīfah on Earth? | **Unit 4: Controlling Our Thoughts** |
| False Piety | Controlling Your Thoughts |
| Superstition | Maintaining a Relationship |
| Do Not Transgress Limits | The Power of Forgiveness |
| Secular and Religious Duties | Reading the Qur'ān |
| Islamic Views on Racism | Afraid to Think, Forbidden to Ask |
| **Unit 5: Principles of Finance in Islam** | **Unit 5: A Review of Key Concepts** |
| Public Finance in Early Islam | Lower Your Gaze |
| Wealth in The Qur'an | 'Ā'ishah (ra): The Child Bride |
| Islamic Investment | "Strike" in Sūrah An-Nisā' |
| Language of Investment | The Myth About the Satanic Verse |
| Faith-Based Wealth Building | How Jesus Became Christ |
| Managing Earning and spending | Rūh and Nafs |
| Leading an Interest Free Life | **Unit 6: Faith-Based Wealth Building** |
| **Unit 6: Islam and the World** | Taking financial control early |
| Islamic Architecture | Fundamental of Finance |
| Islam in Spain and Portugal | Islamic Investment |